Access your Online Resources

All the resources from *Creating an Inclusive Classroom for DLD* are available to download, designed to ensure this book best supports your professional needs.

Go to https://resourcecentre.routledge.com/speechmark and click on the cover of this book.

Answer the question prompt using your copy of the book to gain access to the online content.

Creating an Inclusive Classroom for DLD

Developmental Language Disorder (DLD) affects an average of two children in every mainstream classroom, yet it continues to be a relatively unknown condition. This book equips teachers with a practical toolkit of strategies and resources which will not only support children with DLD but enhance the learning of the whole class.

The book provides a comprehensive introduction to DLD and explores key topics from receptive language and working memory to maximising visuals, supporting transitions and creating an inclusive environment where *all* children can thrive. Each topic contains:

- Practical ideas for working on a whole-class level, as well as targeted and specialist ideas for groups and individuals;
- Guidance on creating a classroom culture where children are listened to and where they feel settled, safe and happy to ask for help;
- Strategies and advice for working with families alongside opportunities to reflect on current practice;
- A wealth of printable resources, templates and examples which can be used to support children with DLD in the mainstream classroom without impacting on teachers' already heavy workload.

Placing a focus on inclusive teaching to enable all children to reach their potential (DLD diagnosis or not), this is an empowering and essential resource for primary school teachers and teaching assistants, as well as speech and language therapists.

Katie Little is a Special Needs Coordinator (SENCo) at an inner-city school in Bradford. She has worked in mainstream primary schools for over 20 years across the Bradford and Keighley area and has been a SENCo for over six years. Katie is passionate about supporting all children with additional needs, particularly those with Developmental Language Disorder. She has previously worked in an outstanding school where she was instrumental in developing pathways, processes, school guidance and training for SEND. Katie champions self-advocacy in students and strives to enable pupils to understand and achieve their own potential, working closely with families and practitioners collaboratively.

'At a time when awareness of Developmental Language Disorder (DLD) is starting to grow in schools, the question turns to "how can we support our students with DLD to learn?" And Katie Little's book fits the bill. Drawing on her experience as a teacher and SENCO, Katie provides a practical and feasible guide. There are hundreds of ideas that will leave the readers thinking "I can do that". But what [she] does extremely well is explain why these methods work. DLD is very common, and so every school needs a copy of this book. And every class teacher needs to be familiar with the content.'

Stephen Parsons, *Chair, RADLD International*

'Whether you are working in education, or a parent of a child who is struggling in school, this book is a must-read. Katie offers informative insight into this common but often undiagnosed condition as well as useful tips and guidance to help pupils with DLD flourish at school and beyond!'

Michelle Blanchard MBE, *Headteacher in the Beckfoot Trust*

'I love this book! It is written from the heart and experience of a teacher who has been on their own journey of understanding and learning about supporting pupils with DLD. The book is packed with real-life examples, scenarios, case studies and strategies that you can start to put into practice in a mainstream classroom tomorrow. This is a MUST-read for all teachers, and the best bit – the strategies will support ALL pupils, not just those with DLD!'

Victoria Wadsworth, *Speech and Language Therapist, Chair of NAPLIC*

'This book is an essential toolkit for teachers looking to better support children with Developmental Language Disorder. With clear explanations, practical strategies and ready-to-use resources, it empowers teachers to create an inclusive classroom environment where all children can thrive. The author's extensive experience as a teacher and SENCO shines through, making this a valuable and accessible guide for mainstream schools. A must-have for any inclusive classroom!'

Shahnaz Bi, *Assistant Principal within the Dixons Academies Trust*

Creating an Inclusive Classroom for DLD

A Teacher's Toolkit to Support Children with Developmental Language Disorder

Katie Little

Routledge
Taylor & Francis Group
LONDON AND NEW YORK

Designed cover image: Getty Images

First published 2026
by Routledge
4 Park Square, Milton Park, Abingdon, Oxon OX14 4RN

and by Routledge
605 Third Avenue, New York, NY 10158

Routledge is an imprint of the Taylor & Francis Group, an informa business

British Library Cataloguing-in-Publication Data
A catalogue record for this book is available from the British Library

ISBN: 9781032717654 (hbk)
ISBN: 9781032717647 (pbk)
ISBN: 9781032717869 (ebk)

DOI: 10.4324/9781032717869

Typeset in DIN Pro
by Deanta Global Publishing Services, Chennai, India

Access the Support Material: https://resourcecentre.routledge.com/speechmark

This book is dedicated to all children with Developmental Language Disorder (diagnosis or not) who are working incredibly hard every day. You are amazing!

And a thank you to all adults who work tirelessly in schools to ensure that children get the very best education and achieve success. You are making a difference.

Contents

About the Author

Katie Little is a Special Needs Coordinator (SENCo) at an inner-city school in Bradford. She has worked in mainstream primary schools across the West Yorkshire area for over 20 years and has been a SENCo for over six years. She has a BA (Hons) degree in Education Studies and Postgraduate Certificates in both 'Primary Education' and in 'Education for Special Needs and Inclusion'. Katie is an Attachment and Trauma Lead, a Senior Mental Health Lead and a Youth Mental Health First Aider.

Katie has been passionate about supporting children with additional needs throughout her career, particularly those with Developmental Language Disorder (DLD). She champions self-advocacy in students and strives to enable pupils to understand and achieve their own potential, working closely with families and practitioners collaboratively. She is currently actively involved in teaching and appreciates the challenges of a busy mainstream classroom and the diverse needs of students accessing the curriculum.

Katie was first introduced to DLD when she worked jointly with a Speech and Language Therapist in a school several years ago. She has previously worked in an outstanding school where she was instrumental in developing pathways, processes, school guidance and training for Special Educational Needs. She is continuing the journey of raising awareness of DLD in her current school and implementing good policy and practice.

Katie regularly presents at conferences and events across the UK on DLD and how to best support children with Speech, Language and Communication needs in a mainstream school. Katie lives in the Bradford area with her husband and her two children.

Introduction

On average, **2–3 children in every mainstream classroom** will have Developmental Language Disorder (DLD) yet it remains relatively unknown within schools. Although being a **lifelong condition** and currently thought to be as common as other, more widely recognised conditions, many teachers have not yet heard of DLD and as a result, often do not have the knowledge or the tools to support these children effectively.

Children with DLD who are not receiving the necessary support in schools can often look to adults as though they are not listening, not following instructions and, in some cases, can present with challenging behaviours. Because DLD is **relatively 'hidden'**, these behaviours can often be misdiagnosed for other conditions.

As someone with over 20 years' experience of teaching primary-aged children and over six years' experience being a Special Needs Coordinator (SENCo) in mainstream schools across the West Yorkshire area, I understand the fast-paced places that schools have become and the pressures that teachers are under every day.

My aim with this book, *Creating an Inclusive Classroom for DLD: A Teacher's Toolkit to Support Children with Developmental Language Disorder*, was not only to provide information about Developmental Language Disorder but also to include **approaches, ideas and practical strategies** to use in educational settings and a **bank of photocopiable resources and templates** which could be implemented immediately, without impacting too much on a teacher's workload.

Throughout this book, I have included some examples of children's experiences to provide a further explanation where required. These examples are not specific to one child but rather a combination of examples drawn from my extensive experience in primary schools, as a SENCo and from working with children who present with challenging behaviours.

The book is broken into the five chapters below:

Chapter 1:	Developmental Language Disorder (Including the signs and the challenges for people with the condition)
Chapter 2:	Classroom Culture and the Learning Environment *(Including strategies to create a safe and happy classroom environment)*
Chapter 3:	Vocabulary Development *(Including the teaching of vocabulary, discussions and good talk and supporting emotional regulation)*
Chapter 4:	The Use of Visuals *(Including classroom displays, visual prompts and scaffolding to support learning)*
Chapter 5:	Transition *(Including how to ensure safety, security and a sense of belonging during times of transition)*

With DLD being relatively unknown, it is unlikely that all children with the condition in schools will have a diagnosis. Therefore, it is vital that educators are looking out for the signs detailed throughout this book and, more importantly, implementing universal strategies to make sure that, diagnosis or not, all children's needs are being met in our classrooms.

All strategies in this book will not only benefit children with Developmental Language Disorder but will benefit *all* children by enhancing high-quality teaching and learning.

Chapter 1

Developmental Language Disorder

What Does this Chapter Cover?

- What is Developmental Language Disorder?
- What are the signs of DLD?
- What challenges do children and young people with DLD face?
- Why is it important to act now and why include universal strategies for all?
- Why is it more prevalent today and what are the challenges that schools face?
- The importance of developing a holistic approach to DLD which includes families and children
- Developmental Language Disorder Awareness Day

What Is Included in the Resources Section?

- DLD Information sheet for families
- Resources for 'Facts on Snacks'
- DLD Bingo game
- DLD Quiz for students
- KS1 Code Breaker activity for DLD Day
- KS2 Code Breaker activity for DLD Day

What Is Developmental Language Disorder?

Developmental Language Disorder (DLD) is when a child or young person has a persistent difficulty in understanding and/or using language. It is not something that a child can 'grow out of' and therefore, can have a lifelong impact. For someone with DLD, support and understanding about their difficulties is required throughout their education and beyond, into adulthood (Speech and Language UK, 2023). '"Developmental" in this context refers to the fact that the condition emerges in

DOI: 10.4324/9781032717869-1

the course of development, rather than being acquired or associated with a known biomedical cause' (Bishop et al., 2017, pp. 1071–1072).

Over the years, this disorder has been known by various terms, including Specific Language Impairment (SLI), but since 2016 has been known as Developmental Language Disorder.

Although it is very common and it is estimated to affect approximately 2–3 children in every class of 30, it is a relatively 'hidden' condition. Despite the prevalence rate of DLD being similar to that of dyslexia and current estimates suggesting that it is up to five times more prevalent than autism (Quigley and Smith, 2023), the majority of teachers may not have heard of it – both the characteristics and the impacts – and therefore may struggle to support these students successfully in the classroom (Glasby et al., 2022).

Reflection: *Had you already heard of Developmental Language Disorder? If you work in a school setting, consider how many members of staff know what DLD is and if you are aware of any children with a diagnosis of DLD?*

What Are the Signs of DLD?

Children and/or young people with DLD can have difficulties in the following areas:

Attention and listening:

Example: *A teacher is introducing an activity in a maths lesson. While they are modelling the activity, there is a child on the front row* ***staring blankly*** *into space. When asked a question, this child is unsure what they have been asked and* ***requires the question repeating****. Once the teacher starts talking again, this child is* ***distracted by equipment*** *on their desk and switches off again. When the activity has been explained and the class are asked to start their work, this child* ***asks the teacher what they need to do****.*

Understanding and receptive language:

Example: *In a science lesson, the teacher is modelling an experiment to test the way forces act on a range of objects on different surfaces. The explanation of the experiment uses a variety of language such as: force, friction, compare, surface, investigate, prediction, measurement, results, table, movement and kinetic energy.*

One child at the front ***nods all the way through*** *the explanation and looks, to the teacher, like she is understanding everything that is being said. She* ***doesn't ask anything*** *when the teacher asks for any questions.*

During the lesson, this child works in a group and ***copies other children*** *but* ***doesn't understand*** *what they are doing, why they are doing it or a lot of the language that is being used. In the next lesson, this child is* ***unable to remember any of the vocabulary or what it means.***

Talking and expressive language:

Example: *In a geography lesson about the rainforest, the teacher is recapping the last lesson and is firing questions to children around the classroom. When one child is asked, they* ***look blank****, and the teacher quickly moves on.*

Later in the lesson, the teacher is asking questions about what they have learnt today and asks the same child another question. This time the child knows what they want to say but ***needs time to formulate an answer*** *and when they do start to answer, their* ***words come out in the wrong order****. The teacher interrupts the child and finishes the sentence for them before moving onto the next question.*

Forming friendships and interacting with peers:

> ***Example:*** *It is breaktime; a group of five children are standing together in the middle of the playground. Four of the children are talking and planning their game and the fifth is* ***standing on the periphery****.*
>
> *Every now and then the fifth child* ***nods and smiles****. Occasionally, the other four children say things to them but they* ***can't formulate an answer fast enough****, and the conversation moves on.*
>
> *Suddenly, the children count down and run away and the fifth child is left* ***looking a little confused****.*
>
> *This child then goes and* ***tells the teacher*** *that this group are being mean to them and not playing with them.*

Literacy skills, reading comprehension and written expression:

> ***Example:*** *A child is in a literacy lesson and has been asked to write a pirate story. They are very excited to do this as they love pirates and have lots of ideas for their work. However, when they come to write,* ***they struggle to start****. They try hard to formulate a sentence in their head to write and drift off, looking blank. They are prompted by the teacher to get started, so they try again but when they write, their* ***sentences are short, some of the words are in the wrong order*** *and* ***they miss grammatical endings off some of the words****.*

Academic attainment:

> ***Example:*** *It is assessment week and children are given tests to measure progress and to assess current levels. One child in the class has been able to read fluently but has* ***not been able to answer the comprehension questions****. They have had* ***difficulty answering language-based maths problems*** *and when they have been given a writing assessment, they took* ***a long time to start it*** *and didn't finish it. The writing they produced was assessed at a low level as they were unable to write longer, more complex sentences, and words were placed in the wrong order. This child was assessed as working roughly two years below their peers.*

What Challenges Do Children and Young People with DLD Face?

When a child struggles with understanding and expressing language, it can have a significant impact on the behaviours that are seen by adults around them. Annison states in her book, *DLD, Why Can't You See Me?* that it is 'more than just "behaviour" you see; further unpicking is key' (Annison, 2022).

Particularly in today's fast-paced, results-driven classrooms, where language is central to the learning process, this unpicking of behaviours is crucial as often teachers and practitioners can misinterpret tell-tale characteristics for other needs (Glasby et al., 2022).

For example:

Academic ability:

In the classroom, most of the learning depends on being able to understand and use language. From a young age, as children are developing, a lot of this language is 'picked up' and learnt implicitly. However, children with DLD struggle with this and require this language to be explicitly taught.

Not being able to process and understand language in the mainstream classroom can give the teacher the impression that the child or young person's academic ability is much lower than their peers which can result in them not being challenged academically and/or being left behind in their learning.

In contrast to this, a child or young person's needs may be masked through a combination of the following: a child may follow or copy other children; they may be over-supported by other adults in the classroom or families may over-help with homework activities. Because of this, the teacher may believe the child is achieving academically when, really, they are being swept along, missing information and not developing a good understanding of what they have done.

Despite these difficulties, children with DLD *can* achieve well at school when the teacher knows that these children learn differently and plan for this.

Behaviour:

Because children with DLD can find it hard to hold information in their head, they can find it challenging to follow instructions. Taking longer to process information, being unable to retain this information or misunderstanding the language used, can easily be misinterpreted as *choosing* to ignore instructions or *deciding* not to listen to the teacher. This can result in the child receiving consequences for their behaviour and being labelled as 'lazy' or 'badly behaved'. 'Many researchers have documented the association between language and behavioural competence' (Hollo, Wehby and Oliver, 2014, p. 170). One study suggested that although mostly unrecognised, 81% of young people who were found to have a social, emotional and mental health need and/or a behavioural difficulty, also had a speech, language and communication need (Hollo, Wehby and Oliver, 2014, cited in Branagan, Cross and Parsons, 2020).

Social Interaction:

As language skills are a vital component when engaging in social interaction, children with DLD can experience difficulties in this area. They can misunderstand language that their peers use, struggle to express themselves clearly with others and can unintentionally communicate in a way that is perceived as disrespectful which, again, can come with consequences including the child being treated unkindly by their peers or being disciplined by an adult, not fully understanding why.

These difficulties can mean that children with DLD can withdraw from social interactions resulting in them having fewer, quality friendships and becoming more 'on-lookers' in their play or choosing to engage in more solitary play. A recent study in America found that '40% of children with DLD in inclusive preschool settings appear to be having significant, problematic relationships with peers' (Chen et al., 2020, p. 13) and that it is 'crucial that early childhood educators attend to the evidence that young children with DLD often have more restricted social networks compared to other children, and they are susceptible to peer rejection and isolation' (Chen et al., 2020, pp. 13–14).

Confidence and self-esteem:

All of these challenges can have a significant effect on a child's self-esteem and confidence as they are working hard to listen, to understand, to follow instructions, to make positive behaviour choices and to show their true abilities but can often feel unseen, unheard and undervalued.

To fully create an equitable classroom for children with DLD, they need to be given the tools to be able to access their learning, to display and celebrate their greatest academic and social abilities, and to reach their full potential.

***Reflection**: After reading the examples above, can you think of any children or young people in your setting who are presenting with these behaviours who could have Developmental Language Disorder?*

Why Is it Important to Act Now and Why Include Universal Strategies for All?

Despite its prevalence and the increasing amount of awareness being raised around DLD, it continues to remain relatively unknown amongst teaching staff in schools. Many of the characteristics of DLD can present like other needs or behaviours and can be misinterpreted in schools (and at home), meaning it is not always flagged up as a language difficulty. As a result, these children can find themselves in the best cases, put into interventions for social skills or emotional regulation groups, but in the worst cases, being reprimanded by missing playtimes or being given detentions and so on.

Historically, if a child presented with a speech, language and communication need (including DLD), they would be referred to a speech and language team and school would wait to hear from them. However, because of the potential challenges and impacts on the child or young person and because of increasingly long waiting lists, it is beneficial to have a good understanding of DLD and to put the support in place immediately.

Because not all children with DLD will have a diagnosis (and in fact currently *most* children with DLD do not have one), this shouldn't mean that they do not get the support they need. The impact of DLD on a child's life can be mitigated by using universal strategies to ensure inclusivity alongside reasonable adjustments (Graham and Tancredi, 2019, cited in Glasby et al., 2022). Therefore, it is essential that educators put the universal strategies in place for *all* children to ensure that we are meeting the needs of every child in our schools.

All the strategies in this book are useful for *all* children as well as those with DLD and will contribute to a safe and supportive classroom with high quality teaching which enhances learning for *all*.

Why Is it More Prevalent Today and What Are the Challenges that Schools Face?

Today's classrooms are extremely fast-paced, and staff face a huge amount of pressure to deliver the curriculum, to prepare children for rigorous testing and to ensure high standards. On top of this, schools are also faced with longer waiting lists to get support from professionals, budget cuts resulting in a reduction of staff and in some areas a gradual increase of need for a variety of reasons.

In a class of 30, with its variety of need, it can be extremely difficult to ensure that *every* child has *all* the provision they need for *every* lesson, and targeted support can tend to be focused on the children who demonstrate the most challenging behaviours. Therefore, as DLD is a hidden condition, it is easy for these children to go 'under the radar'. We must ensure that these children have their needs met in the same way that others do.

DLD is a long-term condition which cannot be cured by a single intervention programme or approach but rather can be supported by universal techniques such as the culture in the classroom, the way new vocabulary is introduced, a focus on extraneous cognitive load being reduced and visuals being used to support language – to list a few.

This book aims to provide a toolkit of these strategies, techniques and photocopiable resources to help teachers to best support these children in today's fast-paced classrooms.

The Importance of Developing a Holistic Approach to DLD which Includes Families and Children

It is vital that awareness of this lifelong condition is developed in schools as it can have a significant impact on a child's education, social interaction, self-esteem and confidence and ultimately their lives as a whole.

If children with DLD do not receive the right support at the right time, they can feel undervalued and believe that there is something *wrong* with them. Even if they do not have a diagnosis, *all* children need to feel valued, need to feel heard and to feel a daily sense of achievement.

Developing self-awareness for the child is important. For those with a diagnosis, this could be exploring what DLD means, the challenges they may face, how to ask for help and how to help themselves. For those *without* a diagnosis but presenting with the same needs, self-awareness remains important – understanding what they find difficult and exploring how they can mitigate against these challenges. This will support these children to develop a more positive view of themselves. They can begin to understand their needs and what helps them but, also, what their superpowers and greatest qualities are.

Because children also spend a lot of time at home, parents, carers and families can have a significant amount of impact on their child and if they are not aware that their child finds language difficult, like teachers, they can also misinterpret this as 'bad' behaviour. Developing this awareness at home is just as vital to support the child. This book includes strategies and resources to educate parents, carers and families about DLD and to help them best support their child at home.

Reflection*: Consider how you involve the children in developing an understanding of their needs and how you include parents, carers and families in your current setting?*

Developmental Language Disorder Awareness Day

Every year there is an official 'DLD day' in the Autumn term which is a great opportunity to develop awareness of Developmental Language Disorder. On the Raising Awareness of Developmental Language Disorder (RADLD) website (https://radld.org), there are lots of ideas for activities for this day that can be used for staff, students and families, including video clips, information sheets, quizzes and many more!

An example of an information sheet about DLD for families and resources that can be used for DLD day can be found in the resources section at the end of this chapter.

Key Takeaways from Chapter 1

- Developmental Language Disorder, although relatively hidden, **affects approximately 2–3 children** in every mainstream classroom.
- People with DLD **struggle in a variety of areas** including attention and listening, receptive and expressive language, literacy skills and social interaction.
- Many of the **behaviours of children with DLD can be misinterpreted** by adults (in school and at home) as other needs e.g., behavioural.
- As DLD currently remains relatively unknown, **universal strategies should be developed** rather than targeted solely for those with a diagnosis of DLD.
- It is important to **take a holistic approach** including families and the child or young person.

References

Annison, S. (2022). *DLD Why Can't You See Me?* Bear With Us Productions.

Bishop, D.V., Snowling, M.J., Thompson, P.A., Greenhalgh et al. (2017). Phase 2 of CATALISE: A multinational and multidisciplinary Delphi consensus study of problems with language development: Terminology. *Journal of Child Psychology and Psychiatry, 58*(10), pp. 1068–1080.

Branagan, A., Cross, M. and Parsons, S. (2020). *Language for Behaviour and Emotions: A Practical Guide to Working with Children and Young People*. Routledge.

Chen, J., Justice, L.M., Rhoad-Drogalis, A., Lin, T.J. et al. (2020). Social networks of children with developmental language disorder in inclusive preschool programs. *Child Development, 91*(2), pp. 471–487.

Glasby, J., Graham, L.J., White, S.L. and Tancredi, H. (2022). Do teachers know enough about the characteristics and educational impacts of Developmental Language Disorder (DLD) to successfully include students with DLD? *Teaching and Teacher Education, 119*, p. 103868.

Hollo, A., Wehby, J.H. and Oliver, R.M., (2014). Unidentified language deficits in children with emotional and behavioral disorders: A meta-analysis. *Exceptional Children, 80*(2), pp. 169–186.

Quigley, D. and Smith, M. (2023). Getting the word out: How teachers can recognise and support children with developmental language disorder in an inclusive classroom. In *The Routledge Handbook of Inclusive Education for Teacher Educators* (pp. 467–482). Routledge India.

Speech and Language UK (2023) *Inclusion by design for children and young people with Developmental Language Disorder (DLD)*. Available at https://speechandlanguage.org.uk/media/3349/ican_dld_guide_final_aug4.pdf [accessed 11 November 2023].

Chapter 1

Resources Section

Developmental Language Disorder

Information Sheet for Families

What Is Developmental Language Disorder (DLD)?

DLD is when a child or young person has a persistent difficulty in understanding and/or using language. It is described as 'hidden' as you cannot tell that a child has DLD by looking at them. It starts in childhood and cannot be 'cured' or 'grown out of' as it is a lifelong condition.

Although some studies have shown that DLD is as common as other, more well-known conditions such as autism, it is relatively unknown. Approximately 2–3 children in every class of 30 will have Developmental Language Disorder.

What Are the Signs of Developmental Language Disorder?

If a child or young person has DLD, they can have difficulties in the following areas:

- Focus and attention
- Listening skills
- Formulating sentences and talking
- Understanding language
- Following instructions
- Literacy skills –reading comprehension and writing
- Forming friendships
- Academic attainment

What Can I Do if I Think My Child May Have DLD?

If your child is struggling with any of the above, speak to your child's class teacher about your concerns. You can also speak to the school's Special Needs Coordinator (SENCo) about a referral to your local speech and language team.

How Can I Help My Child at Home?

If you believe your child may have DLD, below are some things you can do to help them at home:

- Make sure that you **get your child's attention** before speaking to them.
- Ensure that **instructions are clear, simple, given in order** and if necessary, one instruction at a time.
- **Check for understanding** and reassure your child that you understand that they are finding it difficult. Try not to get cross with your child if it seems like they are ignoring instructions.
- When speaking to your child, **allow extra thinking time** for them to think about what you have said and to formulate an answer.
- If your child is taking a while to say something, listen and encourage. **Try not to finish their sentences for them.**

Facts on Snacks
and Other Ideas for Staff and Students

Staff

'Facts on snacks' are a fun way to develop awareness of Developmental Language Disorder and are very simple to do.

Facts are printed onto small pieces of paper and attached to a sweet treat of your choice. When someone chooses a treat, they can also read a fact about DLD. This can be developed further by creating a display in the staffroom where staff can pin their fact up once they have read it. This can remain in the staffroom ll year as a reminder.

Children

There are a number of ways that this could be developed to share facts about DLD with children.

See some below:

- **Pass the fact** – for children, this could be a 'pass the parcel' style game where when the music stops, you pick the fact out of a bag and read a fact.
- **Fact finding** – facts could be placed on a large die and then taken in turns to roll the die and read the fact.
- **Facts snap** – similar to a pairs game, lay facts face down and each child picks two at a time to read and if they are a match, they keep them. The winner is the child who has to most pairs when there are no cards left.
- **Splat the facts** – this is an activity where children stand in the middle of a classroom or hall with two signs labelled 'True' and 'False'. The adult reads a fact about DLD and if it is true the children have to run and touch the 'true' sign and if it is false, they run and touch the 'false' sign then return to the centre for the next fact.
- **Fact sorting game** – children could be given a variety of facts which they could sort into true and false statements.
- **Fact treasure hunt** – facts are hidden around an area (this could be a classroom, a hall, a playground etc.). Children then search the area for facts and record them on a sheet. This could be developed as more of a scavenger hunt where children are given a sheet of questions and a riddle-style location to find the answers.

Facts about DLD

DLD can easily be mistaken for something else so it is described as hidden.

DLD can affect a child or young person's confidence and self-esteem.

DLD is a lifelong condition.

People with DLD can have difficulties with attention and listening.

DLD starts in childhood and continues into adulthood.

People with DLD can have difficulties with understanding language.

DLD affects people all around the world in any language.

People with DLD can have difficulties with talking and expressive language.

DLD is as common as other conditions such as autism.

People with DLD can have difficulties with forming friendships.

On average, DLD affects 2–3 children in each class of 30.

People with DLD can have difficulties with interacting with peers.

DLD can affect a child or young person's success at school.

People with DLD can have difficulties with literacy skills.

DLD stands for developmental language disorder.

DLD is when a person can have difficulty talking and understanding words.

There is no known cause for DLD.

DLD is not something that that a child can 'grow out of'.

DLD can run in families.

DLD affects both children and adults.

You cannot tell if a person has DLD by looking at them.

DLD has been called other names such as Specific Language Impairment (SLI)

DLD can occur with other conditions such as ADHD.

This condition has been known as Developmental Language Disorder (DLD) since 2016.

Support from professionals including teachers can really help people with DLD.

Everyone can help by knowing about DLD.

Attach these to your favourite snacks to create **'Facts on Snacks!'**

DLD Bingo

It lasts all their life 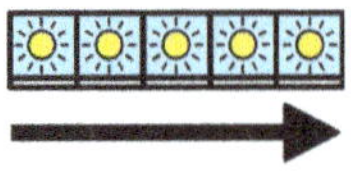	Can affect people in any language 	It can make it difficult to concentrate 
It starts when people are young 	Affects 2–3 children in a class 	Everyone can help by knowing about it 
You can't see it 	It can be difficult to understand words 	Teachers can help 

It can be difficult to understand words 	You can't see it 	Affects 2–3 children in a class 
It can make it difficult to concentrate 	It stands for Developmental Language Disorder DLD	Everyone can help by knowing about it 
Teachers can help 	There is no known cause 	It can affect friendships 

DLD Bingo

Following instructions can be difficult 	It can affect a person's Literacy skills ABC	There is no known cause 
Everyone can help by knowing about it 	It lasts all their life 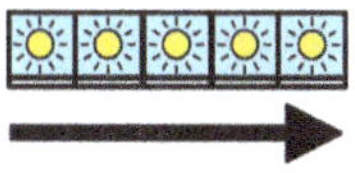	It can affect friendships 
It stands for Developmental Language Disorder DLD	Teachers can help 	It starts when people are young 

It can affect friendships 	It stands for Developmental Language Disorder DLD	It affects people all over the world 
It can affect a person's Literacy skills ABC	There is no known cause 	People can find talking difficult 
Teachers can help 	Can affect people in any language 	Everyone can help by knowing about it 

DLD Bingo

There is no known cause 	People can find talking difficult 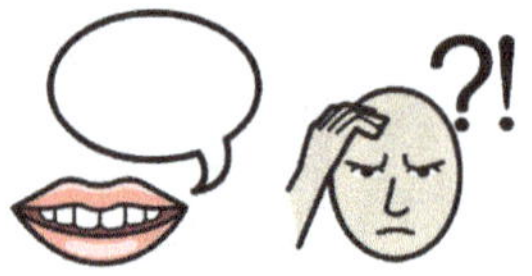	It affects people all over the world 
It can affect a person's Literacy skills ABC	It lasts all their life 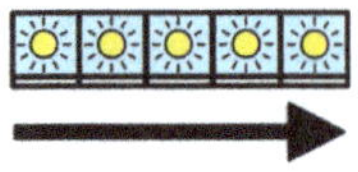	It can make it difficult to concentrate 
Affects 2–3 children in a class 	Can affect people in any language 	You can't see it 

It lasts all their life 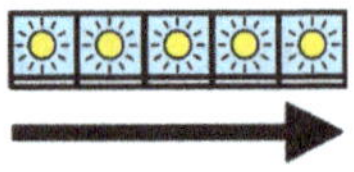	You can't see it 	People can find talking difficult 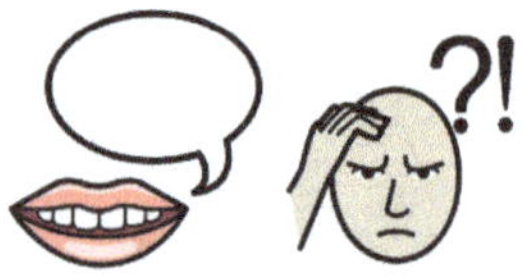
It starts when people are young 	It affects people all over the world 	Affects 2–3 children in a class 
It can affect friendships 	It stands for Developmental Language Disorder DLD	Teachers can help 

DLD Bingo Cards

It lasts all their life 	Can affect people in any language 	It can make it difficult to concentrate 	It starts when people are young 
Affects 2–3 children in a class 	Everyone can help by knowing about it 	You can't see it 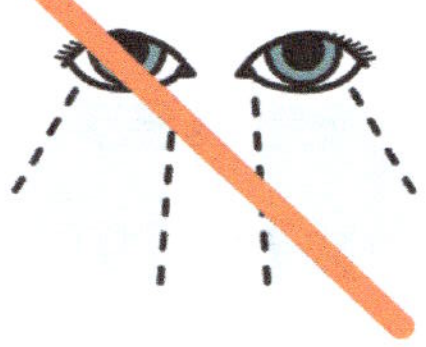	It can be difficult to understand words 

DLD Bingo Cards

Teachers can help 	It stands for Developmental Language Disorder DLD	There is no known cause 	It can affect friendships 
Following instructions can be difficult 	It can affect a person's Literacy skills ABC	It affects people all over the world 	People can find talking difficult 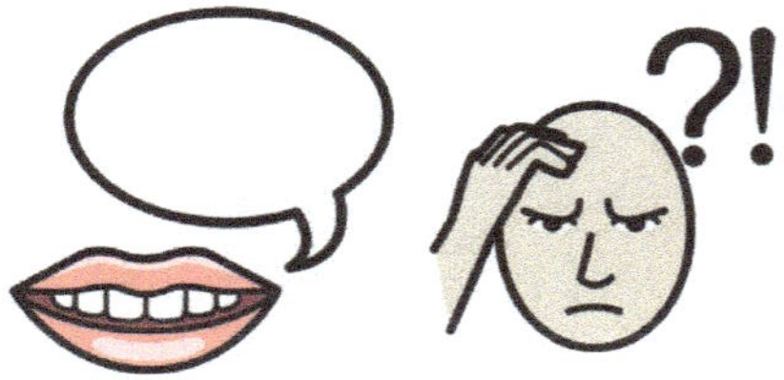

DLD Quiz

For Students

What does DLD stand for?

1. Developmental Literacy Difficulties ☐
2. Developmental Language Disorder ☐
3. Difficulty with a Language Deficit ☐

How long does DLD last for?

1. Only in childhood ☐
2. For 2–3 years ☐
3. DLD is a lifelong condition ☐

Why is DLD described as 'hidden'?

1. It only happens in other countries ☐
2. It is not obvious by looking at someone ☐
3. It is not very common ☐

On average how many children in each class are affected by DLD?

1. Half of a class of 30 ☐
2. Approximately 9–10 children ☐
3. 2–3 children in every class ☐

What difficulties can a person with DLD have? Tick all that apply.

1. Talking ☐
2. Attention and listening ☐
3. Confidence and self-esteem ☐
4. Understanding language ☐
5. Forming friendships ☐
6. Literacy skills ☐

Who can help children with Developmental Language Disorder?

1. Parents, carers and families ☐
2. Teachers and adults in school ☐
3. Professionals like speech and language therapists ☐
4. Everyone ☐

DLD Code Breaker (KS1)

Use the code to find the facts about Developmental Language Disorder

a	b	c	d	e	f	g	h	i	j
14	26	11	20	4	19	12	24	1	25
k	l	m	n	o	p	q	r	s	t
6	23	5	13	7	15	2	17	21	10
u	v	w	x	y	z				
22	8	16	3	18	9				

1. What does DLD stand for?

20	4	8	4	23	7	15	5	4	13	10	14	23

23	14	13	12	22	14	12	4

20	1	21	7	17	20	4	17

2. How many children in each class could have DLD?

10	16	7

11	24	1	23	20	17	4	13

1	13

4	8	4	17	18

11	23	14	21	21

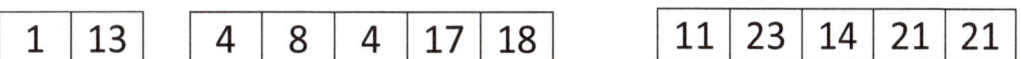

DLD Code Breaker (KS2)

Use the code to find facts about Developmental Language Disorder

a	b	c	d	e	f	g	h	i	j
14	26	11	20	4	19	12	24	1	25
k	l	m	n	o	p	q	r	s	t
6	23	5	13	7	15	2	17	21	10
u	v	w	x	y	z				
22	8	16	3	18	9				

FACT 1: What does DLD stand for?

20	4	8	4	23	7	15	5	4	13	10	14	23

____

23	14	13	12	22	14	12	4

20	1	21	7	17	20	4	17

____

FACT 2: How many children in each class could have DLD?

10	16	7

11	24	1	23	20	17	4	13

____

1	13

4	8	4	17	18

11	23	14	21	21

____

FACT 3: What do people with DLD find difficult?

10	14	23	6	1	13	12

14	13	20

22	13	20	4	17	21	10	14	13	20	1	13	12

16	7	17	20	21

FACT 4: How long does DLD last for?

20	23	20

1	21

14

23	1	19	4	23	7	13	12

11	7	13	20	1	10	1	7	13

FACT 5: Who can have DLD?

14	20	22	23	10	21

14	13	20

11	24	1	23	20	17	4	13

Chapter 2

Classroom Culture and the Learning Environment

What Does this Chapter Cover?

- Creating a safe and secure learning environment
- Creating a positive classroom culture
- Building positive relationships
- Reducing extraneous cognitive load
- Economy of language and extra processing time

What Is Included in the Resources Section?

- PACE Information sheet for teachers
- PACE Scripts for Lanyards
- Reframing Your Language sheet
- PACE Information sheet for families
- Blank Class Rules sheet and an example
- Blank Class Charter and an example
- Social story for 'My Happy and Safe Classroom' and Supporting Sentence Stems
- Communication Card Examples
- Fact File
- Building Relationships Top Tips sheet for families
- Social story for 'My One-to-One Time'
- Social story for 'Managing Strong Feelings and Emotions'
- Morning Routine sheet with visuals
- Bedtime Routine sheet and with visuals
- Reward Chart
- Social story for 'Going to the Supermarket'
- Social story for 'Mealtimes'
- Social story for 'Sleeping in My Own Bed'
- Economy of Language scripts for families
- Social story for 'Using Less Language'

DOI: 10.4324/9781032717869-2

Creating a Safe and Secure Learning Environment

A classroom which is inclusive and supportive of any additional needs is beneficial for *all* students. Creating this whole class culture and 'a positive and supportive environment for all means placing support for pupils with SEND at the heart of school priorities—being inclusive by design' (Davies and Henderson, 2020, p. 10).

Constructive and positive daily interactions are vital in ensuring that the students feel safe and valued. This presence and experience of safety has a profound effect on pupils, and we need to consider how educators and school systems can both aggravate or calm stress, and work towards negating these factors (Bombèr and Hughes, 2013).

As adults working in schools, it is easy to fall into doing things that have *always been done here* and believe that everything possible is done to create this environment for our students. However, even the most skilled practitioners can benefit from regular prompts, reflection and ultimately a fine-tuning of their skills (Branagan, Cross and Parsons, 2020).

The PACE Approach

Over 20 years ago, Dr Daniel Hughes developed a trauma-informed approach known as PACE (**P**layfulness, **A**cceptance, **C**uriosity and **E**mpathy). Rather than an 'intervention', this approach is a basic 'way of being' and is based primarily on building trusting relationships and developing a sense of security. It is a way of communicating with a child or young person when faced with any unwanted behaviour. This could be anything from being late to a lesson, to appearing not to be listening, to being in crisis and displaying challenging behaviours.

This approach is broken down into the following four areas:

Playfulness: Many schools have become serious places due to the fast-paced and ever-increasing curricular demands and it is important that practitioners give each other permission to smile, laugh and to be playful (Bombèr and Hughes, 2013). This part of the approach is about creating a fun, light and playful atmosphere when communicating with the child, using a light tone or a 'story-telling' voice, rather than a seemingly irritated or lecturing tone.

When practitioners are playful with the child, it strengthens the relationship: it shows that they care about the child, that they will be there for them no matter what and can enable the child to build trust so they will come to them again in the future (Bombèr and Hughes, 2013). Reacting to the child or young person in this way can instantly diffuse a situation and communicates to the child that the adult is on their side (or on their 'team') and has their best interests at heart. This can be used in several ways depending on both the chronological age and the developmental age of the child.

Playfulness example:

Scenario: *A child in Year 3 is in a maths lesson and when the teacher walks around the classroom, they haven't yet completed any of the independent task.*

Without playfulness:
Teacher: Why haven't you even started?
Child: <Shrugs>
Teacher: Did you listen when I gave the instructions?
Child: Yes.
Teacher: Then why haven't you done it?
Child: Don't get it.
Teacher: Well then, you should have been listening. I haven't got time to go around everyone individually and tell them again!

With playfulness:
Teacher: <Name>, you haven't started yet, do you need help? <in a light, soft and playful tone>
Child: <Nods>
Teacher: Do you understand what to do?
Child: No.
Teacher: <Smiling> Come on, let me show you again and we can do the first part together.

In the first example, the teacher communicates to the child a number of things: that the child has *chosen* not to listen to the instructions; that the teacher is cross with them for not starting the work yet and that they are not 'worth' the teacher's time to sit down and show them again. This approach can have a significant effect on the child's confidence and self-esteem and will ensure that this child will not ask for help in the future.

In the second example, the teacher keeps the tone light and asks what *they* can do to help. They offer to repeat the instructions and work *with* them so they understand it.

This communicates to the child that they are not to blame; that it is okay to ask for help and that the teacher values them. This builds self-esteem and means that they will be more likely to ask for help in the future.

Acceptance: This is about being accepting and non-judgemental when speaking to the child. It is important to validate the child's feelings and let them know that it is normal to feel them. This approach does not mean that shocking, unacceptable or dangerous behaviours should be overlooked but rather acknowledging and accepting that the child hidden beneath the behaviours needs to be seen and heard (Bombèr and Hughes, 2013).

Unconditional, continuous and clear acceptance creates safety for the students and is fundamental in maintaining strong relationships with value and meaning (Bombèr and Hughes, 2013). By showing acceptance and saying sentences such as, 'I can see that you are angry and that is okay', you are validating the child's feelings. At this time, it is also a good opportunity to start to narrate and name the feelings that the children may be feeling both emotionally and physically.

Acceptance example:

Scenario: *It is playtime and a group of children have just run up to the teacher in the playground to say that a child has pushed one of them. The child who is accused of pushing, runs up to the teacher and starts shouting.*

Without acceptance:
Teacher: Why did you push <Name>? You know we don't do mean things like that at our school!
Child: <Shouting> We were playing tig so I tigged him!
Teacher: Stop shouting at me, otherwise you will have to miss some playtime! Why did you push, that is an unkind thing to do?
Child: <Getting more frustrated> I was playing tig and everyone was doing it!
Teacher: You have really hurt <Name>, say sorry to them.
Child: But ... it was the game!
Teacher: Say sorry!
Child: <Shouts> Sorry! <Runs away>

With acceptance:
Teacher: <To the child> What happened?
Child: <Shouting> We were playing tig so I tigged him!

Teacher: So, you were trying to play the game with your friends?
Child: Yes!
Teacher: <To the child> I'm really happy that you are playing with your friends. In the game of tig though, only the person who is 'on', can tig people. When you were 'tigging' your friend, I think you accidentally did it a little hard. Next time, when you tig someone, try and be a little more gentle.
Teacher: <To the group of friends> <Name> didn't mean to hurt anyone, she was playing the game and misunderstood the rules. She understands now.
Child: <To her friends> Sorry, can we play again?

In the first example, the teacher communicates that they think that the child did it on purpose; that they are letting the school down or that she doesn't fit in with the school because 'We don't do that here' and the child is made to say sorry when she still doesn't understand what she did wrong. This scenario resulted in the child becoming upset, not understanding what she did wrong and playing alone.

In the second example, the teacher takes time to ask what happened from the child's point of view. They try to get to the bottom of the problem without judging the child for the secondary behaviour (shouting). By showing understanding and acceptance, the situation is automatically diffused, and the child feels listened to, valued and understood. This scenario resulted in the child now understanding the game, the friends understanding why it happened, a sorry was given from the child rather than forced and the friends continued playing together.

Curiosity: One of our greatest gifts we could ever give someone is that of our empathetic curiosity (Bombèr and Hughes, 2013, p. 122). Often children and young people struggle to open up if directly questioned, for example: *Why didn't you listen the first time? Why are you shouting? Why haven't you completed your work?* This part of the PACE approach is about being curious about the child's behaviour in a less confrontational way. It is about questioning and wondering about the reasons out loud. At this stage, an answer is not always required from the child, for example: *I wonder if you didn't sleep well last night*, or *I wonder if you didn't understand the instruction I gave*, and so on.

Curiosity example:

Scenario: *A reception child is refusing to sit down with his class on the carpet for a science lesson. An adult tries to encourage him to sit down but he runs away from them and hides in the cloakroom.*

Without curiosity:
Teacher: What is going on?!
Child: Nothing! <Runs away>
Teacher: <Name>, you need to come back and sit on the carpet.
Child: No! <Runs and hides>
Teacher: You have 5 seconds to sit back on the carpet.
Child: No!
Teacher: 5...4...3...2...1, right you will have to miss some playtime and we will have to speak to your parents about this behaviour.

With curiosity:
Teacher: Is everything okay?
Child: Yes! <Runs away>
Teacher: I wonder why you are finding it hard to sit on the carpet today.
Child: <Silence>
Teacher: I wonder if you are finding the work difficult.
Child: <Shouting> No!
Teacher: Hmm, I wonder if you have had a fall out with a friend.
Child: <Looks at the teacher> Wasn't my fault!
Teacher: Tell me about it and let's sort it out together.

In the first example, the teacher communicates that their primary goal is to get the child to sit down rather than to find out what the matter is and that if they do not do as the adult asks, there will be a consequence. This approach can escalate a problem.

In the second example, the child still cannot communicate what they are upset about but this time, the teacher 'wonders' out loud until she gets to the root of the problem. The child sees that the teacher cares and wants to help them. This approach can diffuse the situation while developing a positive and trusting relationship between the student and the teacher.

Empathy: 'Our pupils need to experience our empathy if they are to experience value, understanding, safety, and the desire to learn when they are with us' (Bombèr and Hughes, 2013, p. 142). This is about the adult putting themselves in the child's shoes and communicating to the child that they really understand. It is at this point that the adult can tell the child that they are not alone, that they understand and that they can work the problem out together.

It is important to note the difference between 'sympathy' and 'empathy'. Sympathy is when someone feels sorry for someone without really connecting with the feelings that are associated with their situation. It can be a challenge for adults in schools to remember what is feels like to be a child and the things that were important to them at that time and therefore can easily dismiss a child's situation by saying things like: 'Oh well, we all fall out with people sometimes' or 'Well life isn't fair!'

Empathy is actually being able to put yourself in that person's shoes, being there with them and letting them know you are there to listen. If we don't listen to what we consider to be the little, insignificant things, the child will learn not to share their feelings when it is a *big* thing. To them, all of these situations are big, cause strong emotions and require an adult to support them.

Empathy example:

Scenario: *A Year 6 child is in a history lesson about World War 2. The activity is to read a text about the topic and answer questions about it. The teacher has just finished giving the instructions.*

Without empathy
Child: <Calls out to the teacher> Sir, what were we meant to do again?
Teacher: I have literally just told you, now get on with the task.
Child: But I don't get it.
Teacher: Then you should have listened.
Child: <Throws their work on the floor and swears>
Teacher: <Sends the child to the head teacher>

With empathy
Child: <Calls out to the teacher> Sir, what were we meant to do again?
Teacher: <Goes over to the child and speaks quietly> Would you like me to go over it again with you?
Child: <Shouting and throwing work on the floor> I don't get it!!

Teacher: I can see that you are angry and I know how bad that can feel. When I feel angry, my stomach hurts and I can feel like I want to throw things too.
Child: <Stares at the table>
Teacher: <Picks up the work> Shall I go through it with you and we can do the first one together?
Child: <Nods>

In the first example, the teacher is communicating to the child that they have done something wrong by not listening and that they are not willing to help. This forces the child to either ask a friend or copy them, not complete the work at all or become angry or upset. The result of this scenario is the child being reprimanded for the secondary behaviour, missing the learning and not feeling valued.

In the second example, the teacher takes accountability for the learning and understands that the child needs the task explaining again. They understand, accept and empathise with the child that they feel frustrated rather than reprimanding them for it and they show the child that they are: (a) supporting them no matter what and (b) they want to help. The result of this scenario is that the child feels valued and understood, they see that their teacher is on their 'team' no matter what and that the teacher can empathise with how they are feeling. It is likely in a situation like this that the child will still feel frustrated, but this adult knows that it is a 'big ask' for the child to calm down so quickly and that it may take a bit of time.

Implementing the PACE approach on a universal level can ensure that all children feel valued, understood and listened to which is vital in creating a safe and productive learning environment.

Targeted/Specialist Strategies

Children with DLD in the mainstream classroom can appear as though they are not listening, are *choosing* not to follow instructions, are not trying or are lazy, and may be reprimanded for this but they are often trying really hard. With playfulness, acceptance, curiosity and empathy, the children in our classes can feel valued, listened to, heard, understood and can flourish.

Although the PACE approach is fundamentally a 'way of being' in the classroom, there will likely be times when there are children who require this approach on a more targeted/specialist basis. As we know, behaviour is a form of communication, and these behaviours could be communicating an unmet DLD need.

When used effectively, the PACE approach can have a significant effect on a young person. Having trusted adults around them who are accepting, empathetic and who see the best in them, ensures that they do not feel continually on 'high alert' but instead are happy, feel safe and are settled to learn which enables them to reach their full potential. See the case study below:

CASE STUDY:

A key stage 2 student at an inner-city school in the North of England was struggling in the classroom. He presented with some extreme behaviours, had received eight suspensions from November to March for physical assault and persistent disruptive behaviour and was receiving multiple red cards on a daily basis. There were a number of factors that contributed to this:*

- *A social and emotional need (including attachment difficulties) due to being a child looked after (CLA).*
- *Due to the COVID pandemic, he had not been in school on a full-time basis since his reception year.*
- *A possible underlying speech, language and communication need (although there was no diagnosis).*

Behaviours seen in school included:

- *Verbal aggression (including shouting, name calling, threatening language and swearing).*
- *Physical aggression (including trying to strangle other students, biting, punching, kicking adults and children, kicking/ throwing and drawing on furniture and class-room items).*
- *Leaving the classroom, running away and hiding.*
- *Not following instructions.*
- *Refusing to complete learning tasks (sometimes shouting that they were too hard).*

Strategies put in place to support this student:

- *The PACE approach was used when communicating with this student.*
- *This child had a team of adults who he knew were on his 'team' and who he knew would be accepting, understanding, empathetic and non-judgemental.*

- *Regular check-ins were put in place to communicate to this student that the adults cared about him and to also create opportunities for him to communicate anything that was worrying him.*
- *Regular checks in were done before tasks to check that he didn't need any further explanation or support.*
- *Although this student was capable of completing the whole class tasks, shorter bursts of learning were given with the purpose of allowing him to be successful daily and develop his confidence and self-esteem.*
- *Interventions to explore emotions were implemented.*

The outcome: *This student is now settled for the majority of his time in school; he stays in the classroom all day and accesses his learning alongside his peers. He is working within age-related expectations across the board and the outlook for him is positive. Within this time, this student has received only a handful of red cards and has not been suspended since.*

**Red cards are a 'consequence' for difficult behaviour which involves Senior Leadership support.*

This method, as most things, is not a quick fix but instead a long-term approach. Teachers can often fall into the trap of trying an approach for a month or two and then concluding that it doesn't work. For children who present with challenging behaviours such as this student, it is likely that it will take a significant amount of time to build a trusting relationship and to demonstrate to the child that no matter how much they push the boundaries or what behaviours are seen, the adults are not going anywhere.

Without taking the PACE approach, the outcome for the student above could have been significantly different.

Parents, Carers and Families

Sharing this information with parents, carers and families can be beneficial to ensure that the approach is consistent across home and school. This can be done in a number of ways, including information sheets, meetings/workshops, individual meetings about specific children and regular posts on the school communication lines for example.

Resources to support the PACE approach including examples of how to re-frame your language, scripts for staff lanyards, and information sheets for both staff and families can be found in the resources section at the end of this chapter.

Reflection: *When reading the examples above, does it make you think of any children you have worked with? Are these scenarios familiar? Consider how you could use the PACE approach next time you are faced with these types of situations.*

Creating a Positive Classroom Culture

Children with DLD can have difficulties with processing information, formulating sentences, understanding language and developing vocabulary which can make the fast-paced mainstream classroom an overwhelming place to be. Developing a positive culture in the classroom where children can confidently and openly say that they haven't understood something, that they don't know what a word means, that they need longer to process information, or to make mistakes can benefit not only those with DLD, but *all* children.

As adults in the classroom, it is important to listen with your full attention, to give children the time they need to speak (Branagan, Cross and Parsons, 2020), to explicitly *teach* sentence starters to use in class, for example: 'I didn't understand ...' or 'I'm confused about ...' and then to respond in a supportive, non-judgemental way. If attempts to ask for help are met negatively, this could prevent the child from asking in the future.

Here are several ways to develop a positive culture in the classroom:

Class rules: It can be useful to create a set of class rules both for the children *and* for the adults in the classroom. For example:

Rules for the children can include	• To listen when others are speaking • To be respectful of other people's opinions • To ask for help if needed • To be supportive if others ask for help • To engage in learning and ask lots of questions
Rules for the adults can include	• To give adequate processing/thinking time • To speak slowly and clearly and include visuals with instructions • To provide any resources and visuals needed to best support children with their learning • To always respond in a non-judgemental way

Having class rules for the adults, as well as the children, and developing these rules together with the class, promotes a trusting, two-way relationship built on mutual respect; it ensures that the students feel heard and develops a positive classroom culture where all children can thrive.

Encouraging and listening to pupil voice can support the development of this safe, positive and productive classroom environment where everyone is a team working *together* to achieve goals rather than the teaching being something that is *done to* the students. There are many ways that pupil voice can be collected for this. For example, during a DLD Awareness Day, one school asked the children in KS2 to give their teachers some tips on how to best support them in class.

Here are some examples of the children's ideas:

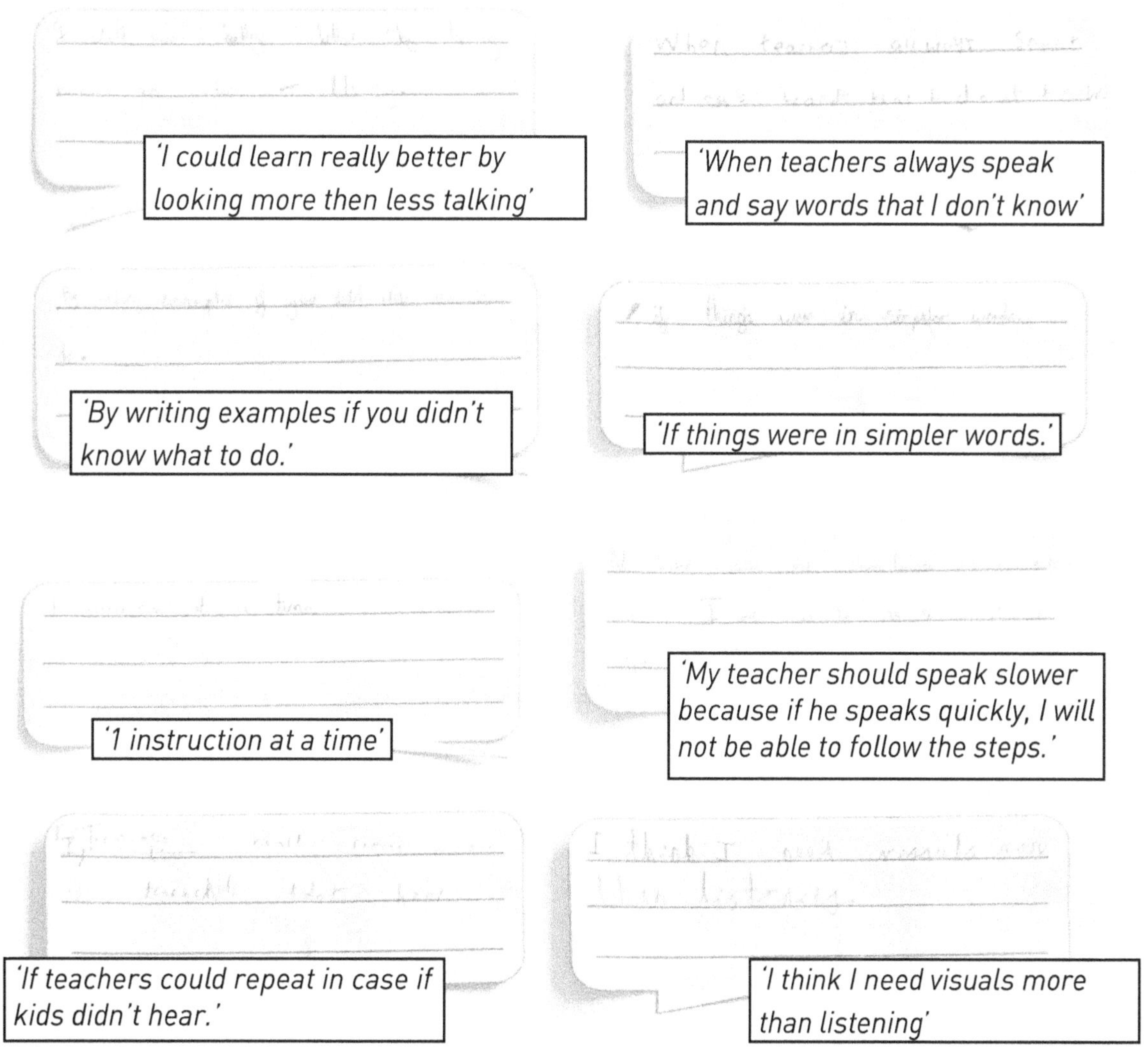

'I could learn really better by looking more then less talking'
'When teachers always speak and say words that I don't know'
'By writing examples if you didn't know what to do.'
'If things were in simpler words.'
'1 instruction at a time'
'My teacher should speak slower because if he speaks quickly, I will not be able to follow the steps.'
'If teachers could repeat in case if kids didn't hear.'
'I think I need visuals more than listening'

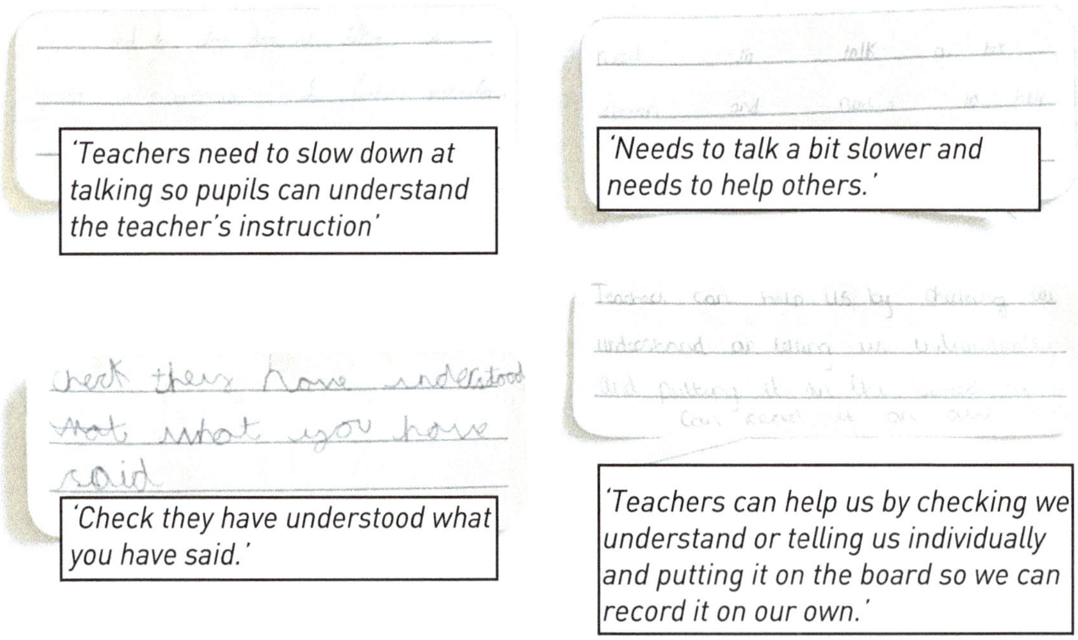
'Teachers need to slow down at talking so pupils can understand the teacher's instruction'
'Needs to talk a bit slower and needs to help others.'
'Check they have understood what you have said.'
'Teachers can help us by checking we understand or telling us individually and putting it on the board so we can record it on our own.'

Completing activities such as this can support the creation of class rules and/or a class charter.

A class charter: Similar to class rules, a charter can be created at the beginning of an academic year and involves working together as a class to write a set of rules or *promises* that the class (including adults) have agreed to.

A whole class/whole school social story (Gray, 2015): A social story can be used universally to reassure all children that it is okay to ask for help, to say that you don't understand or to ask for an instruction to be repeated. Using this social story has several purposes.

1) It gives children *permission* to ask for help and can provide the talk stems to structure their questions or comments.
2) It reminds the rest of the class how to respond if someone asks for help, e.g. to be supportive and not to laugh.
3) It inadvertently models to the teacher how to respond when children ask for help. It is very easy as a teacher to tell the student that they mustn't have been listening and it takes practice to respond in a more positive way.
4) Over time, when read regularly, the culture in the classroom should shift to a positive, more productive environment where children feel safe enough to make mistakes and ask questions, and where they can make the progress that they have the potential to do.

It is beneficial to read this social story regularly throughout the year, to keep reminding children (and adults). However, reading the social story alone will not have the impact. For this culture to fully thrive in a classroom, this concept should be referred to daily through constant verbal reminders and referring to displayed talk stems and/or visuals to help children to structure sentences to ask for help.

Whole-class check-ins: Checking understanding is a vital part of the teaching and learning process. Extra checks can also be really useful to use while the classroom culture is developing for students who may still not always feel comfortable to ask in front of the class – or at all. Examples of how this can be done include: using taught actions or gestures, for example thumbs up/down, coloured cards or visuals on tables which students can turn over to communicate that they need to ask a question and physically walking around the classroom at the beginning of a lesson to 'check' everyone is okay and knows what to do.

Targeted/Specialist Strategies

Because children with DLD may find that they have more questions than others in the class and may find that there is more vocabulary that they don't understand, they can lack the confidence to openly ask for help and therefore may require more than the universal offer to support this. Working towards a positive classroom culture where all children feel comfortable to speak up can be a journey and for some children and it may be necessary to add in some more targeted/specialist strategies and create smaller, more achievable steps along the way. For example:

- Pre-teaching vocabulary and/or concepts so they have knowledge about the topic and have the opportunity to ask any questions they may have prior to the lesson.
- Providing resources in lessons to provide extra support, e.g. word banks with visuals, extra information about the lesson and task plans etc.
- Once the independent task has started, have an *extra* check-in with these students to ask them one-to-one whether they need any further explanations or need anything explaining again.
- Some children may respond well to having an alternative method of communicating to the teacher that they need help without having to put their hand up e.g. a colour coded card that can be turned to red if they want an adult, a card that says 'I'm okay' on one side and 'I need help' on the other side (words or visuals depending on the child).

- Feedback sessions after the lesson – a one-to-one catch-up session to give the child the opportunity to say if they didn't understand something.

Parents, Carers and Families

Parents, carers and families of children with DLD may benefit from support with developing a positive culture at home and from being given information about the following concepts:

- Not all the language/ vocabulary used at home may be understood and may need further explanation and/or teaching. Families can be supported to check understanding and to encourage their child to ask about any words or concepts that they have not understood.
- Children with DLD can struggle to hold instructions in their head. Families may need support in understanding this and understanding the best way to give instructions to their child, e.g. only giving one instruction at a time or using visuals to support the instructions etc.
- Formulating sentences can be a challenge for children with DLD and so they benefit from being given time to express themselves. Families would benefit from developing knowledge about processing time and understanding why this is important.

Blank templates and examples of class rules and a class charter can be found in the resources section at the end of this chapter along with an example of the whole class social story ('My Happy and Safe Classroom'), including the talk stems and supporting visuals for display, and communication cards for children to signal that they need help.

Reflection: *Consider how often pupil voice is collated in your current educational setting and whether you feel that the students you work with would feel happy and supported to ask for help.*

Building Positive Relationships

'Effective teaching and learning requires positive relationships and interactions between teachers and pupils' (Davies and Henderson, 2020, p. 11). It is vital for interpersonal safety to be present if an open and engaged manner of relating and learning is maintained which is at the heart of all successful education (Bombèr and Hughes, 2013).

There are many ways that positive relationships can be developed on a universal level, below are some examples:

- Positive praise strategies, e.g. verbal praise, high fives, thumbs up.
- Using techniques to develop confidence and self-esteem, e.g. ensuring that learning tasks are matched closely to the children's needs (not too easy but not too challenging).
- Developing mutual respect, e.g. being able to say if you as the adult have made mistakes, saying sorry if appropriate, listening to the children when they speak and understanding that what is seemingly a small thing can be a very important thing to them.
- Being consistent and fair to all, *really* listening when the students talk to you and taking the time to explore the reasons behind any behaviours.
- Developing a sense of belonging within the classroom/school and getting to know all students as individuals.
- Making the learning environment fun and somewhere where making mistakes is accepted and valued in the learning process.

Targeted/Specialist Strategies

Although it is important to have these positive relationships with *all* children, there are inevitably going to be smaller groups or individuals who require a more targeted/specialist approach. In their 2019 guidance report on 'Improving Behaviour in Schools', the Education Endowment Foundation (EEF) discuss promising results from a small study which involved intentionally focusing on children who require more intensive support to develop those essential relationships. They highlight strategies to establish, maintain and restore positive relationships, including ensuring that there is a 5-to-1 ratio of positive to negative interactions (Rhodes et al., 2019).

For these children, as well as the universal strategies above, the following strategies are also helpful to support these relationships:

Keeping the children in mind: To support a positive relationship, it can be really powerful to let children know that you are thinking about them, that you care about them and are keeping them in mind. This can be achieved in several ways:

- In September, giving these children a quick call to say that you are looking forward to seeing them for the new academic year.
- Remembering activities that the children have told you that they are doing at the weekend and asking them about them, e.g. *Did you have a good time at your friend's birthday party?*
- Remembering any holidays that they are having and asking how they went.
- Remembering information about the children, e.g. names of siblings/ pets etc. and asking them about them.
- Knowing what these children need in class to help them with their learning and providing it, e.g. a task plan, visuals, extra check-ins, a fidget toy, regular breaks, short burst of learning, a separate work station etc.

Knowing what is a 'big ask': This concept involves making reasonable adjustments for children who find certain aspects of the school day and environment challenging. For children with DLD, school life can be overwhelming, and it can require a lot of energy and concentration to be able to do all the things that are expected of them. Knowing what is a 'big ask' is about prioritising targets for these children and somewhat 'overlooking' other aspects. See below for examples of this:

- If a child finds it challenging to listen to instructions as part of a whole class group, not expecting them to follow the instruction but instead planning to give them individual instructions afterwards.
- If they have completed their work but have misunderstood what to do, not becoming frustrated with this child for not listening but instead understanding, reassuring them and showing them again.
- If a child is asked a question and is finding it difficult to organise their thoughts to formulate an answer, not rushing them, finishing an answer for them or moving on to another child but instead making reasonable adjustments such as giving a talk stem for them to finish, giving them longer to answer or pre-warning them with the questions so they have an answer ready.
- If a child has seemingly been unkind to another child, not assuming that they are in the wrong but instead giving the child time to regulate before speaking to them and then using talk stems and/or a learnt script to support them to explain what happened.

- If a child is becoming frustrated in a lesson because they are finding it challenging, not reacting to the secondary behaviour and giving a consequence or 'time out', but instead giving them 'time in' and listening to them and their frustrations.
- If a child is struggling to concentrate for the entirety of the whole class input on the carpet, not expecting them to sit for long periods of time but, instead, giving them a different activity at this time and then giving them an individual input afterwards.
- If a child finds it challenging to complete the whole task that the rest of the class are expected to do, make the task shorter for this student or make it clear that the focus is the quality of the task and not the quantity.

Parents, Carers and Families

Support for home:

Many children experience positives relationships at home as well as in school. However, there will also be some who require extra support with this. To support these families, the following strategies could be used:

- Providing top tips to developing positive relationships at home.
- Social stories for different aspects of home life, e.g. experiencing quality one-to-one time with family, helping with homework and how to manage strong emotions etc.

Support for school:

Fact files: It can be useful to involve families and find out more about individuals and their past. Information covered could include the early years and milestones, what they enjoy and are good at, what they find difficult and any traumatic events they have experienced. This can highlight specific needs and/or can explain children's triggers which can then be utilised in the classroom to ensure that the children feel settled, valued and understood.

An example of a fact file, a 'Top Tips' sheet for families about building positive relationships and examples of social stories for one-to-one time and managing strong emotions can be found in the resources section at the end of this chapter.

Reflection: *Think about what you currently do in school to build positive relationships. Can you think of any students who may benefit from a more targeted approach?*

Reducing Extraneous Cognitive Load

There has been much documented over the years about cognitive-load theory which looks at the relationship between working memory and the long-term memory and aims to explain how the information processing load generated by learning tasks can affect a person's ability to process and learn new information, and to transfer this knowledge into the long-term memory (Sweller, Merrienboer and Paas, 2019).

A person's working memory is the ability to temporarily hold information in their heads with the purpose of then manipulating and using that information. As humans, our working memory capacity is limited and therefore we can only process a limited amount of information at a time.

A child's cognitive load can increase if:

- information is delivered in an unfamiliar and/or an illogical order
- too much new information is being given
- the topic or information is unfamiliar/new to the child
- there are distractions in the environment including displays, too many resources or noise
- the child has low self-esteem and if they negatively self-talk
- the child is not emotionally regulated at the time of the task and are 'consumed by intrusive worries about failure' (Paas and Merrienboer, 2020, p. 397).

As working memory capacity is so limited, practitioners should ensure that learning tasks are designed in such a way that the available working memory capacity is efficiently used. Environmental barriers can be removed by incorporating universal design principles to maximise learning opportunities for all and then using accessible teaching strategies to minimise extraneous cognitive load and optimise student comprehension (Glasby et al., 2022). By making sure that learning activities don't overburden working memory and teaching strategies to cope with demanding tasks (Quigley, Muijs and Stringer, 2018), children can achieve the highest possible return for their efforts (Paas and Merrienboer, 2020).

Classroom Environment and Displays

As well as the learner themselves and the learning task that they are being asked to complete, the learning environment also can have an effect on cognitive load and its management (Paas and Merrienboer, 2020). To support this, it is useful to consider the following:

- Elaborate and eye-catching displays can be distracting for all children and can consume working memory resources. Empirical studies have shown that 'children in the decorated classroom were less likely to stay focussed and attained lower test scores than children in a classroom without decoration' (Paas and Merrienboer, 2020, p. 397).
- Noise has also been considered 'as a typical irrelevant environmental stimulus that takes limited working memory resources away from the learners' cognitive process' (Paas and Merrienboer, 2020, p. 397).
- Cluttered work areas, whether this be the classroom tables or an individual workstation, can impose on cognitive load and attempts to keep learning areas clear and clutter-free should be made to support this.

Routines

Developing consistent and well-rehearsed routines in the classroom can reduce cognitive load for the students. As skills become more automatic and require less mental effort, there is less imposition on cognitive load (Anderson, 1995, cited in Feldon, 2007), thus freeing up their working memory space for learning tasks.

Universally, this can include routines for the following:

- Timetables: it reduces cognitive load if the child knows what *always* happens on a Monday for example.
- Having the same activities for certain parts of the day, e.g. a morning routine, getting ready for lunchtime and a home time routine. Cognitive load is further reduced if these routines are also displayed visually.
- Transitions: this includes transitioning within the classroom, e.g. from carpet to tables and back and transitioning to lining up for breaks/ lunches etc. This can be done in a number of ways, e.g. signals, counting, sounds etc.
- For stopping children, e.g. hands up, ringing a bell or a clap routine for example, ensuring that every time that is heard, it is time to stop.
- Tidying up – a signal can be given signalling that it is time to tidy up, e.g. a certain song, a timer, a sound etc.

- Structure of lessons, e.g. always having the same structure including aspects such as starter tasks, paired worked, modelled learning, independent task and final task etc.

Targeted/Specialist Strategies

Students with Developmental Language Disorder can struggle with verbal working memory, meaning that they can find it difficult to hold information in their heads and require targeted support with this.

Explicitly teaching certain activities to groups and/or individual students which they can repeat daily, only changing a very small aspect each time, means that their working memory capacity is freed up for the learning as they know the task well. For example:

- Handwriting practice: the letters or words could be printed on the sheet or could be simply written on post it notes as long as it is the same method/procedure every day.
- Writing: use the same format every day such as a picture, some lines to write on, a prompt for what to include (e.g. capital letter, full stop etc), a word bank of high frequency words and two challenge words to include for example.
- Times table/arithmetic practice: use the same number of questions, same style of questions but different numbers.
- For focus: a routine of using a timer for certain activities supported with a visual could be used, e.g. in a morning, the 10-minute timer is used for fine motor activities.
- 1, 2, 3 activities: for example, always having a times table activity for number 1, a familiar maths activity for number 2 and a colouring sheet for number 3.
- Procedures: for writing the date and the title in their books, have a prompt permanently on the table of any child or groups of children who struggle to remember. You can also teach little phrases to help them remember, e.g. 'Name, date and date's on the board!'
- Visuals for routines e.g. putting coat on, going to the toilet, etc.

Parents, Carers and Families

Educating and supporting the families of children with DLD about working memory and cognitive load is beneficial. Below are some examples of how this could be done:

- Morning/ bedtime routine visuals to support children at home and having the same routine every day.
- Social stories for routines e.g. going to the supermarket, mealtimes at home.
- Doing the same things on the same day e.g. always shopping on a Monday.

Examples of morning and bedtime routine charts, social stories for families and a reward chart can be found in the resources section at the end of this chapter.

> ***Reflection:*** *Consider how much of children's cognitive load is taken up in your setting with colourful and engaging displays, busy tables, and the regular introduction of new activities. How could this be reduced to free up working memory capacity?*

Scaffolding

'Scaffolding' is a metaphor for temporary support that is removed when it is no longer required (Davies and Henderson, 2020, p. 26) and has a place in the classroom to support a reduction in cognitive load for students. There are many ways that all teachers use scaffolding in their day-to-day teaching to support all children including explicit instruction, modelling, breaking learning down into manageable chunks, using real-life and concrete resources, using visual prompts, use of talk partners, explicit teaching of vocabulary and time for children to practice the concept or skill independently with focused support where required. Everyone has a limit to their working memory capacity and 'the use of structured planning templates, teacher modelling, worked examples and breaking down activities into steps' (Quigley, Muijs and Stringer, 2018, p. 19) can ensure that it is not used up by extraneous information rather than the task itself.

When considering working memory capacity in the classroom, it is helpful to consider how much *new* information is being introduced and how many steps are involved to enable the children to complete the task and then to provide scaffolding to support these steps.

For example, in maths, when teaching the new concept of finding a fraction of a number, consider what prior knowledge and information will be needed to complete this and (a) ensure that they have had prior teaching on these concepts and (b) provide visual information or prompts so they do not have to hold all this information in their heads.

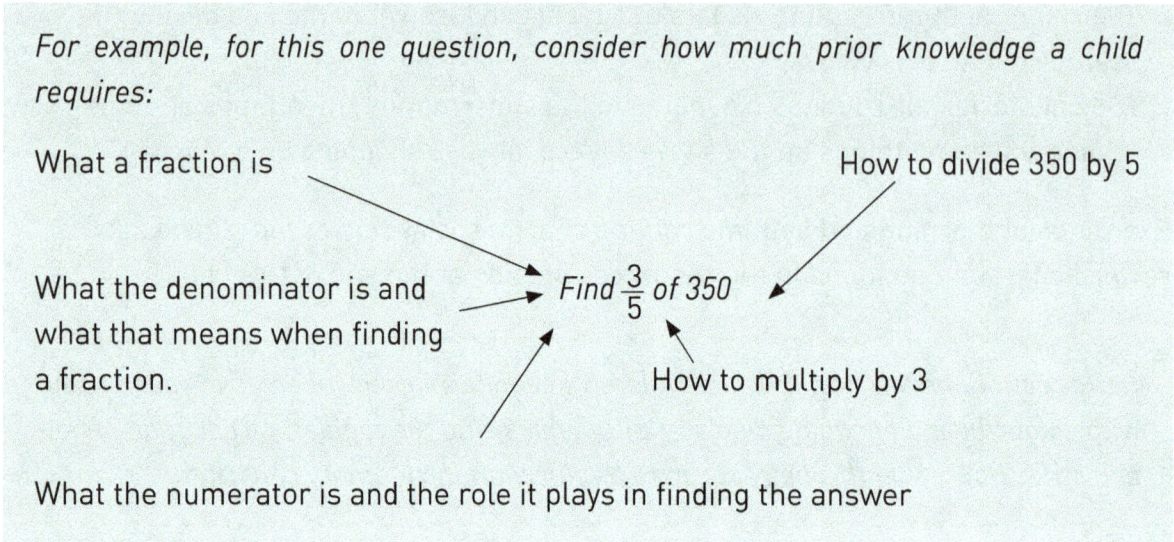

For example, for this one question, consider how much prior knowledge a child requires:

What a fraction is

How to divide 350 by 5

What the denominator is and what that means when finding a fraction.

Find $\frac{3}{5}$ *of 350*

How to multiply by 3

What the numerator is and the role it plays in finding the answer

Targeted/Specialist Strategies

Although these universal strategies are beneficial for all students, some children, particularly those with DLD, will require further scaffolding and practitioners should consider the following to support them:

- Be clear what the students specific target is for the lesson and ensure that it is only this, that the student needs to concentrate on (including handwriting) and then provide scaffolding/supports for the rest.
- That supporting resources, e.g. writing frames, word banks, task plans, are not too 'busy' and only have the required information on. Although it may make the sheet 'look' nicer, any colourful pictures and unnecessary extras can just become a distraction and cause cognitive overload.
- That only the supports that are needed are out in the learning area because having too many can again cause cognitive overload. One way of overcoming this can be to have resources that students 'choose to use', e.g. word banks of their specific words in the back of their book which can be folded out if needed or task plans folded down in the back which can be lifted out when required. Alternatively, your classroom could have a 'support station' where students can choose to select what they need for the activity they are completing.

- How much work the student should be given for one task. It can cause cognitive overload to be faced with a sheet full of calculations, for example, and instead, the student would benefit from having the task broken down into smaller, more manageable chunks on separate sheets which can be accessed once the activity has been completed, but not expected.

Reflection: *Consider how much scaffolding is put in place for those students who need it in the setting that you work in and what consideration is given to working memory and cognitive load when introducing new topics.*

Economy of Language and Extra Processing Time

Something that most teachers and practitioners can be guilty of sometimes is using too much language at a time when less language is required. For example, if a child is dysregulated and is lashing out, adults around them may think that they are doing the right thing by *over*-explaining to them what has happened, why they shouldn't be acting in that way and what will happen if they don't stop the behaviour. Maintaining economy of language when dealing with unwanted behaviours or giving instructions not only supports understanding but also 'helps you conserve your time, words and energy' for more academic instruction (Lemov, 2021).

Similarly, if a child is not understanding something in a lesson, the teacher can be forgiven for thinking that what is required is a further, more detailed explanation when what is needed are fewer words, spoken with clarity to avoid cognitive overload and a feeling of overwhelm.

Adults in the classroom are very skilled at asking high level, targeted and open-ended questions during the learning process to develop their students' learning and to encourage higher level, critical thinking. However, what teachers do *after* they have asked the question is equally, or even more important (Wasik and Hindman, 2018).

All children require processing time throughout all aspects of the school day. However, students with DLD can not only struggle to process the information given but can also find it difficult and time consuming to formulate an answer. Therefore, these students require a much longer processing time and will also benefit from prompts or visual supports. The following strategies will support all children on a universal level:

Questioning:

- Allowing up to 10 seconds' response time.
- Having the question on the board to refer to if required.
- Providing talk stems to structure answers if needed.
- Allowing children to make notes to support their answer.

Learning tasks:

- Plan in extra discussion/thinking time to plan what they will do – especially for writing tasks.
- Prioritise quality not quantity as it may take a child with DLD longer and so they may not produce as much as other children.
- Provide sentence stems or writing frames to support the student to structure their sentences.

Friendship and interaction difficulties:

- Allow a 'calm down' time to process what has happened.
- Provide talk stems to support the structure of preceding discussions.
- Give extra time for the child to formulate an answer when having discussions.

Targeted/Specialist Strategies

As children with DLD struggle with working memory capacity, processing information and formulating sentences, extra thought must be given by adults in school about the language used (how much as well as the level of vocabulary) and the amount of processing time which is given for these children. The strategies below can help with this:

Economy of language:

- Keep instructions short and clear (with visual prompts where appropriate).
- Give instructions one at a time.
- For a longer set of instructions, provide a visual prompt to support.
- Use of scripts for certain times, e.g. when/if emotionally dysregulated.

Processing time:

- Pre-warn children with DLD of any questions that they will be asked and allow them to make notes to refer to.
- Provide talk stems/sentence stems to support the child to structure their responses.
- Provide the question written down so they can refer to it if needed.
- Give extra processing time for the child to respond to any questions.

Parents, Carers and Families

As with staff in school, adults at home can also use too much language, thinking that they are explaining something in detail to their child and would benefit from being explicitly taught to use less language and to give extra processing time. A script for promoting economy of language and a social story for using less language can be sent home to support with this.

Both of these can be found in the resources section at the end of this chapter.

Reflection: *Think about the children that you work with in your settings. How much language is used with them daily? Consider how long you would usually wait after asking a question before prompting them, finishing their sentence for them, or moving on to ask another child.*

Key Takeaways from Chapter 2

- Creating **a safe and happy environment** in the classroom where children feel valued, supported and are encouraged to ask and answer questions (with enough processing time to respond) and free to make mistakes as part of the learning process, benefits *all* children.
- PACE (Playfulness, Acceptance, Curiosity and Empathy) supports a safe environment and helps to develop **positive relationships** based on mutual respect and trust.
- The importance of **educating and supporting families** to understand their child's needs and how best to communicate and support their child at home.
- Consider **pupils' views** both when creating things like class rules and charters but also listening to the little things so they feel comfortable to share the bigger things if they arise.
- The consideration of **extraneous cognitive load**, how it impacts a child's working memory and how to reduce it through the use of routines, scaffolding, economy of language and considering the learning environment.

References

Bombèr, L.M. and Hughes, D.A. (2013). *Settling to Learn: Settling Troubled Pupils to Learn: Why Relationships Matter in School.* Worth Publishing.

Branagan, A., Cross, M. and Parsons, S. (2020). *Language for Behaviour and Emotions: A Practical Guide to Working with Children and Young People.* Routledge.

Davies, K. and Henderson, P. (2020). Special Educational Needs in Mainstream Schools. Guidance Report. Education Endowment Foundation.

EEF (2019). Improving Behaviour in Schools: Guidance Report. Education Endowment Foundation. Available at https://educationendowmentfoundation.org.uk/education-evidence/guidance-reports/behaviour [accessed 7 April 2024].

EEF (2018) Metacognition and Self-Regulated Learning. Guidance Report. Education Endowment Foundation. Available at: https://educationendowmentfoundation.org.uk/education-evidence/guidance-reports/metacognition [accessed 7 April 2024].

Feldon, D.F. (2007). Cognitive load and classroom teaching: The double-edged sword of automaticity. *Educational Psychologist*, *42*(3), pp. 123–137.

Glasby, J., Graham, L.J., White, S.L. and Tancredi, H., (2022). Do teachers know enough about the characteristics and educational impacts of Developmental Language Disorder (DLD) to successfully include students with DLD? *Teaching and Teacher Education*, *119*, p.103868.

Gray, C. (2015). *The New Social Story Book. Revised & Expanded. 15th Anniversary Edition*. Future Horizons.

Lemov, D. (2021). *Teach Like a Champion 3.0: 63 Techniques that Put Students on the Path to College*. John Wiley & Sons.

Paas, F. and van Merriënboer, J.J. (2020). Cognitive-load theory: Methods to manage working memory load in the learning of complex tasks. *Current Directions in Psychological Science, 29*(4), pp. 394–398.

Sweller, J., van Merriënboer, J.J. and Paas, F. (2019). Cognitive architecture and instructional design: 20 years later. *Educational Psychology Review, 31*, pp. 261–292.

Wasik, B.A. and Hindman, A.H. (2018). Why wait? The importance of wait time in developing young students' language and vocabulary skills. *The Reading Teacher, 72*(3), pp. 369–378.

Chapter 2

Resources Section

PACE

(Playfulness, Acceptance, Curiosity and Empathy)

Information Sheet for Teachers

Playfulness:

- A light, playful tone
- Non-confrontational
- A fun and playful atmosphere
- A 'story-telling voice'
- With a smile
- Strengthens relationships
- Can diffuse intense situations

Do you think I can fit under that table with you?

Have you not eaten your Weetabix this morning?

Acceptance:

- Accepting the child and their emotions
- Non—judgemental
- Validates children's feelings
- Strengthens relationships
- Unconditional and clear acceptance
- Narrates feelings

I can see you are feeling angry.

I can see you are finding it hard, can I help?

Curiosity:

- Wondering out loud
- Exploring why children may feel/ be behaving in a certain way
- Not putting the child on the spot
- Showing the child that you care and want to help
- Strengthens relationships

I wonder if you are cross about getting the question wrong.

I wonder if you didn't sleep well last night.

Empathy:

- Putting yourself in the child's shoes
- Empathising with how they are feeling
- Showing the child that you understand
- Understanding the importance to the child of a seemingly small event

I understand how you feel.

I can see why you are feeling so upset

PACE

Scripts for Lanyards

These scripts can be printed and laminated to attach to lanyards.
(For in lessons).

I can see that you are...
(e.g. trying hard, not sure what to do, finding it difficult)

Would you like me to...
(e.g. repeat the instruction, explain it again, come and help you?)

What else can I do...
(e.g. to help, to make it easier to understand, to support you?)

I can see that you are...
(e.g. trying hard, not sure what to do, finding it difficult)

Would you like me to...
(e.g. repeat the instruction, explain it again, come and help you?)

What else can I do...
(e.g. to help, to make it easier to understand, to support you?)

I can see that you are...
(e.g. trying hard, not sure what to do, finding it difficult)

Would you like me to...
(e.g. repeat the instruction, explain it again, come and help you?)

What else can I do...
(e.g. to help, to make it easier to understand, to support you?)

I can see that you are...
(e.g. trying hard, not sure what to do, finding it difficult)

Would you like me to...
(e.g. repeat the instruction, explain it again, come and help you?)

What else can I do...
(e.g. to help, to make it easier to understand, to support you?)

I can see that you are...
(e.g. trying hard, not sure what to do, finding it difficult)

Would you like me to...
(e.g. repeat the instruction, explain it again, come and help you?)

What else can I do...
(e.g. to help, to make it easier to understand, to support you?)

I can see that you are...
(e.g. trying hard, not sure what to do, finding it difficult)

Would you like me to...
(e.g. repeat the instruction, explain it again, come and help you?)

What else can I do...
(e.g. to help, to make it easier to understand, to support you?)

PACE

Scripts for Lanyards

These scripts can be printed and laminated to attach to lanyards.
(For behaviour).

I can see that you are...
(e.g. feeling cross, angry, tired, frustrated etc)

I wonder if...
(e.g. you didn't sleep well, have fallen out with a friend, are finding the work difficult)

I understand what it feels like...
(e.g. when you are tired, when you fall out with someone, when something is hard)
How can I help?

I can see that you are...
(e.g. feeling cross, angry, tired, frustrated etc)

I wonder if...
(e.g. you didn't sleep well, have fallen out with a friend, are finding the work difficult)

I understand what it feels like...
(e.g. when you are tired, when you fall out with someone, when something is hard)
How can I help?

I can see that you are...
(e.g. feeling cross, angry, tired, frustrated etc)

I wonder if...
(e.g. you didn't sleep well, have fallen out with a friend, are finding the work difficult)

I understand what it feels like...
(e.g. when you are tired, when you fall out with someone, when something is hard)
How can I help?

I can see that you are...
(e.g. feeling cross, angry, tired, frustrated etc)

I wonder if...
(e.g. you didn't sleep well, have fallen out with a friend, are finding the work difficult)

I understand what it feels like...
(e.g. when you are tired, when you fall out with someone, when something is hard)
How can I help?

I can see that you are...
(e.g. feeling cross, angry, tired, frustrated etc)

I wonder if...
(e.g. you didn't sleep well, have fallen out with a friend, are finding the work difficult)

I understand what it feels like...
(e.g. when you are tired, when you fall out with someone, when something is hard)
How can I help?

I can see that you are...
(e.g. feeling cross, angry, tired, frustrated etc)

I wonder if...
(e.g. you didn't sleep well, have fallen out with a friend, are finding the work difficult)

I understand what it feels like...
(e.g. when you are tired, when you fall out with someone, when something is hard)
How can I help?

Re-framing your Language

...for listening and understanding.

Original sentence		PACE approach
You should have been listening.	→	I can see you are not sure, would you like me to explain it again?
Why haven't you done as I asked?	→	Do you know what to do? Shall I come and help you with it?
You need to put a bit more effort in.	→	I can see you are trying hard, how can I make it easier for you?
I have already told you. You should have listened.	→	Would you like me to repeat the instruction?

...for fall outs with peers.

Original sentence		PACE approach
Why did you hit them?	→	You are obviously very angry and that's okay. Shall we talk about it?
I haven't got time for these little arguments.	→	I really want to listen to what you have to say. Can we do it at the end of the lesson?
No one will want to play with you if you say or do unkind things to them.	→	I know you are a really good friend so when you are angry, let's find a different way for you to calm down.
How dare you speak like that to me!	→	I wonder if you are upset about something, let's talk about it and see if we can help you feel better.

...behaviour.

Original sentence		PACE approach
What did you do that for?	→	I can see you are angry. Would you like to talk about it?
Who do you think you are talking to?	→	I really want to hear what you have to say, I will come and find you at break time.
Get out from underneath the table.	→	I understand what it feels like to be angry, and I know it doesn't feel good.
That behaviour is not acceptable.	→	I really want to help you, let's solve the problem together.

PACE

(Playfulness, Acceptance, Curiosity and Empathy)

Information Sheet for Families

PACE is an approach or a '*way of being*' with your child which promotes a positive relationship and can help diffuse challenging situations

Playfulness: Spoken in a light, playful tone with a smile, even if faced with angry or strong emotions.

'You seem angry, how can I help?'

'Oops, did you get out the wrong side of the bed this morning?' (with a smile)

Empathy: This is putting yourself in your child's shoes and showing them that you understand how it feels.

'That must feel really bad, I know I don't like that either.'

'I can see why you feel so upset.'

Acceptance: Being non-judgemental and showing that you understand your child's emotions.

'I can see that you are upset/angry'

'I understand that it is difficult to focus when you are frustrated.'

Curiosity: Rather than asking direct questions, wonder out loud.

'I wonder if you are feeling tired today.'

'I wonder if you are upset because you are coming to the supermarket with me.'

Class____Rules

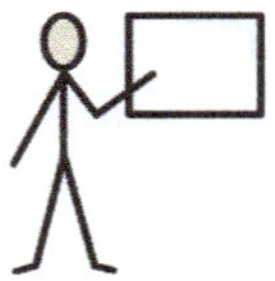

Teachers will...

•

•

•

•

Children will...

•

•

•

•

Class 3 Rules

Teachers will ...

- Check that everyone understands
- Use visuals when giving instructions
- Be understanding
- Make lessons interactive and fun!

Children will ...

- Be respectful
- Always ask for help if they need it
- Be curious and ask lots of questions
- Try their best

Class Charter

In class ___, ____________________________________

____.

The teachers will...

-
-
-
-

The students will...

-
-
-
-

Signed ....

Class Charter

In class 3, we want to feel safe and happy in our classroom.

The teachers will...

- Check that everyone understands
- Use visuals when giving instructions
- Be understanding
- Make lessons interactive and fun!

The students will ...

- Be respectful
- Always ask for help if they need it
- Be curious and ask lots of questions
- Try their best

Signed... Class 3 staff and students...

My Happy and Safe Classroom

We all come to school to learn.

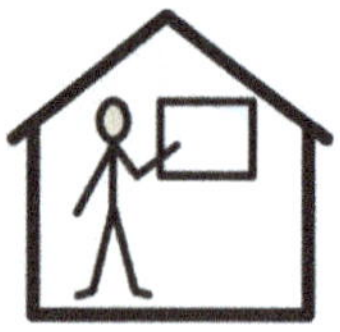

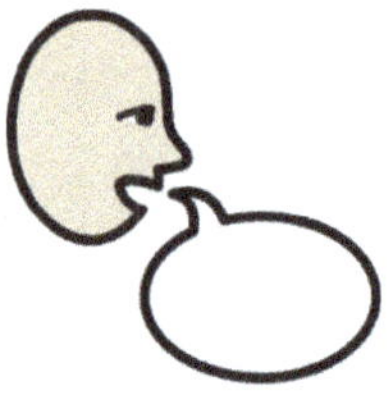

Sometimes my teacher will say things that I don't understand straight away.

This is okay.

Sometimes I won't understand what my teacher wants me to do.

That is okay.

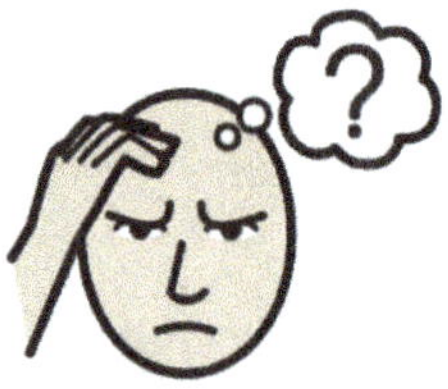

If I don't understand something, I can tell my teacher.
I can say things like:

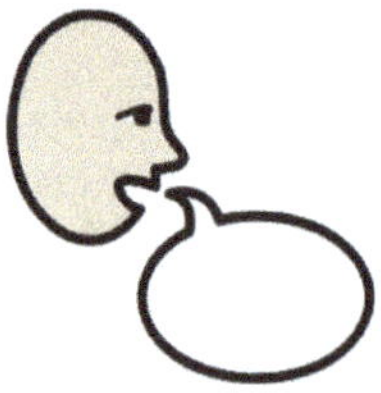

'I don't understand.'

'I'm confused.'

'Can you tell me that again?'

If I say this, my teacher will know that I am trying my best and I just need a little more help.

It will help my teacher if I say exactly what I need help with.
I can say things like:

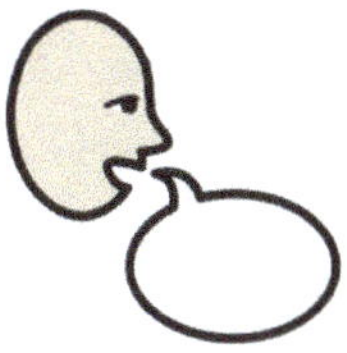

'I don't get the bit about...'

'I understand the bit about...but not the rest.'

'What do you mean by...?'

'What does the word ...mean?'

'You said too much, please tell me one bit at a time.'

If I hear someone ask these questions, I will be understanding and will not laugh at others.

If I ask a question, I know that my teacher and my friends will also be understanding and will not laugh.

We know that no one understands things all of the time and it is okay to say that we don't know something.

We can all work together in our classroom to help each other and to make sure everyone can learn!

If I don’t understand something in class, I could say:

I don’t understand…

I’m confused …

Can you tell me that again?

It will help my teacher if I say exactly what I need help with:

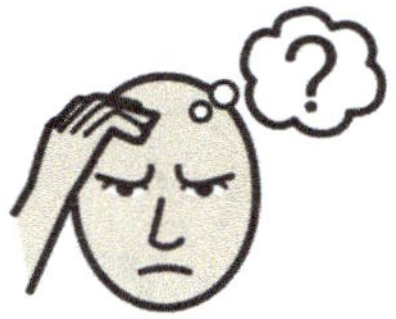

I don’t get the bit about...

I understand ... but not ...

What do you mean by...?

What does the word ... mean?

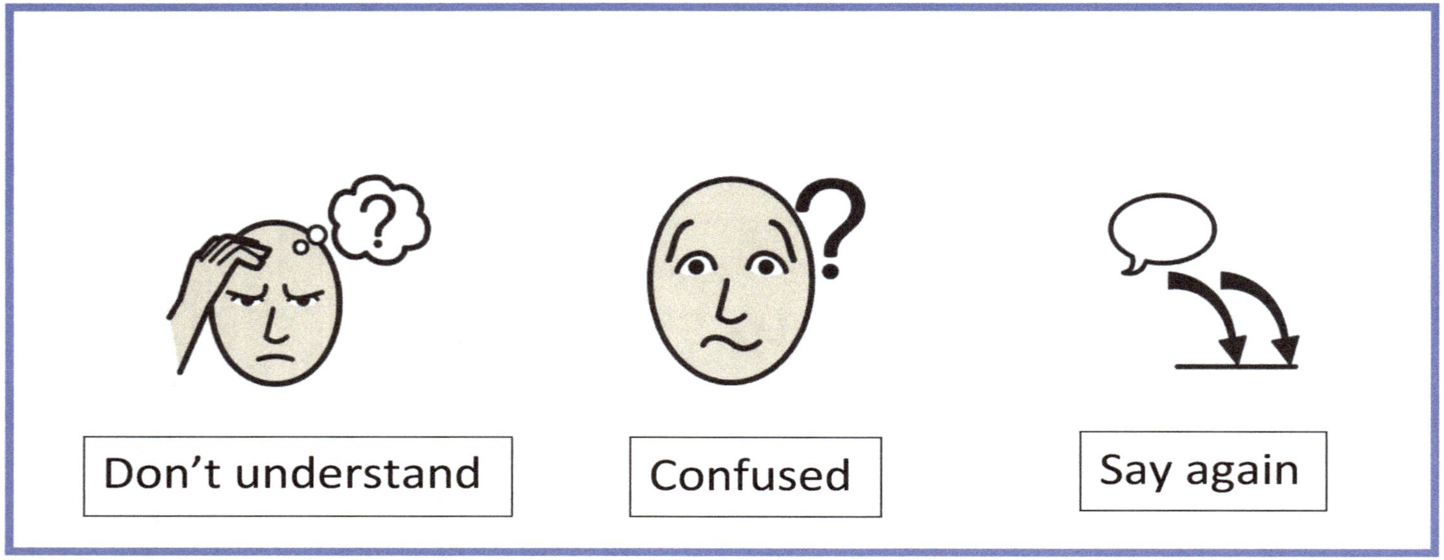
Don’t understand
Confused
Say again

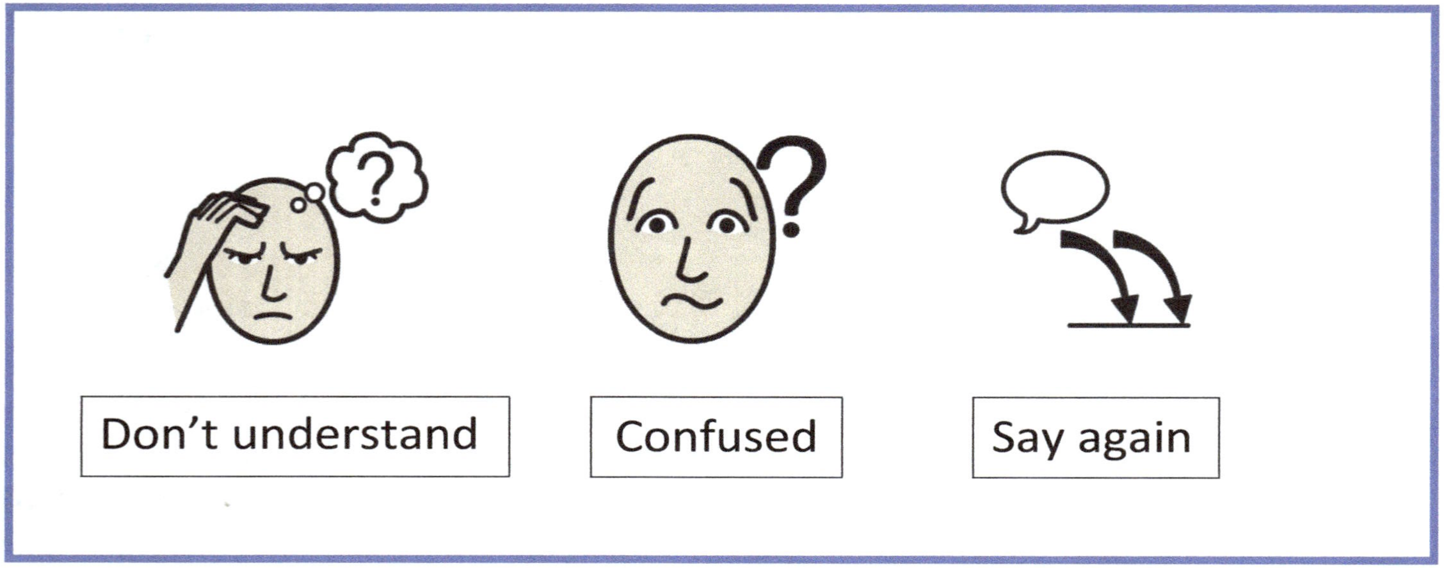
Don’t understand
Confused
Say again

Communication Card Examples

The following cards can be cut out and laminated back-to-back.

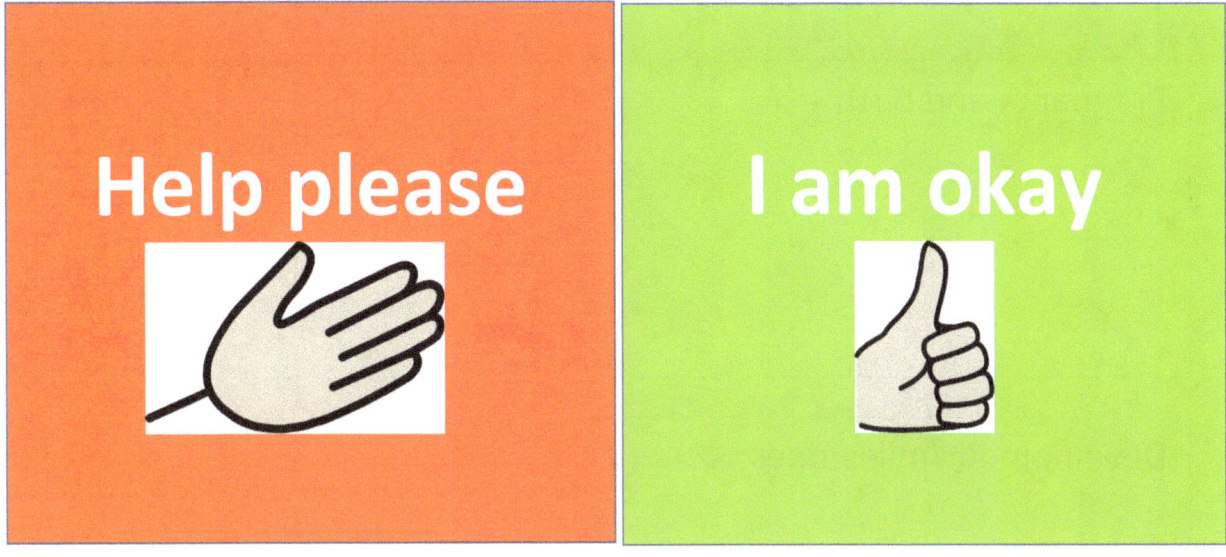

Help please 	**I am okay** 

The following can be cut out and stuck to the table for children to either point to or place something on to communicate non-verbally to the teacher.

Help please	I have a question	I am okay

Help please 	I have a question 	I am okay 

Fact File

Name:

DOB:

Pregnancy and birth:

Development/milestones:

Family: Who lives at home? Who are important people to them?

What is your child good at and what do they like?

What does your child struggle with? What are their dislikes?

Fact File

Main triggers and calmers:

Key events in their life so far (positive and negative):

Any other information about your child:

Building Relationships

Top Tips for Families

Actively **listen** to your child when they tell you things – even if they seem unimportant.

Set clear and consistent **boundaries** and know that it is okay to say no.

Celebrate your child daily and ensure that this praise outweighs any negatives.

Plan **for quality time** with your child with no other distractions.

Acknowledge any feelings and emotions your child has and let them know it is okay to feel that way.

Be a positive role model and encourage open **communication** with your child.

My One-to-One Time

Adults are very busy and have lots of things to do.

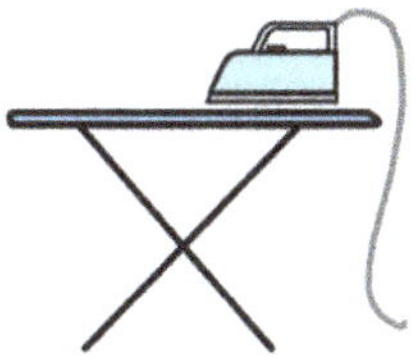

Sometimes I will need to do things by myself. I will try hard not to come to my adult at these times.

There will be a time every day when I get to spend time with my adult. We will spend time together, talk and play together.

My adult will tell me when my time is.

I will enjoy my time with my adult.

Managing Strong Feelings and Emotions

There are lots of different feelings and emotions including feeling happy, sad, excited, angry, confused, frustrated and jealousy. Everyone experiences these different feelings and emotions.

Most of the time, I can manage my emotions but sometimes I need help with this.

If I am feeling a very strong emotion, I can talk to my adults at home about it. It is okay to have this feeling and it is good to talk about it.

When I feel like this, my adults will be understanding and listen to me while I talk –even if I am shouting.

My adult will let me know that it is okay to have strong feelings and will help me to find an activity to help me to feel calm again.

If I talk to my adults when I feel this way, they will feel happy and it will make me feel happy too.

Morning Routine

(Tick)	(Tick)	(Tick)	(Tick)	(Tick)

Name ....

Cut out the cards you need and add to the routine sheet.

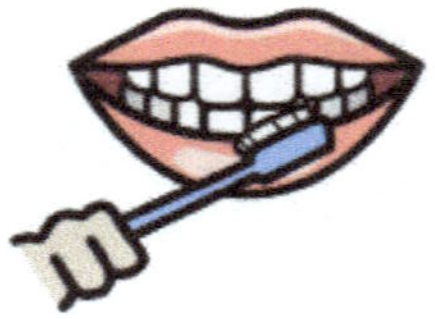
Brush teeth

Toilet

Bath

Get washed

Get dressed

Shoes on

Go to school

Breakfast

Pray

Well done

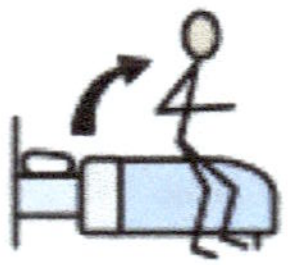
Get out of bed

Read a book

iPad time

Shower

Get school bag

Bedtime Routine

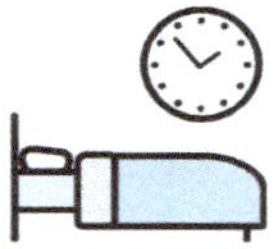

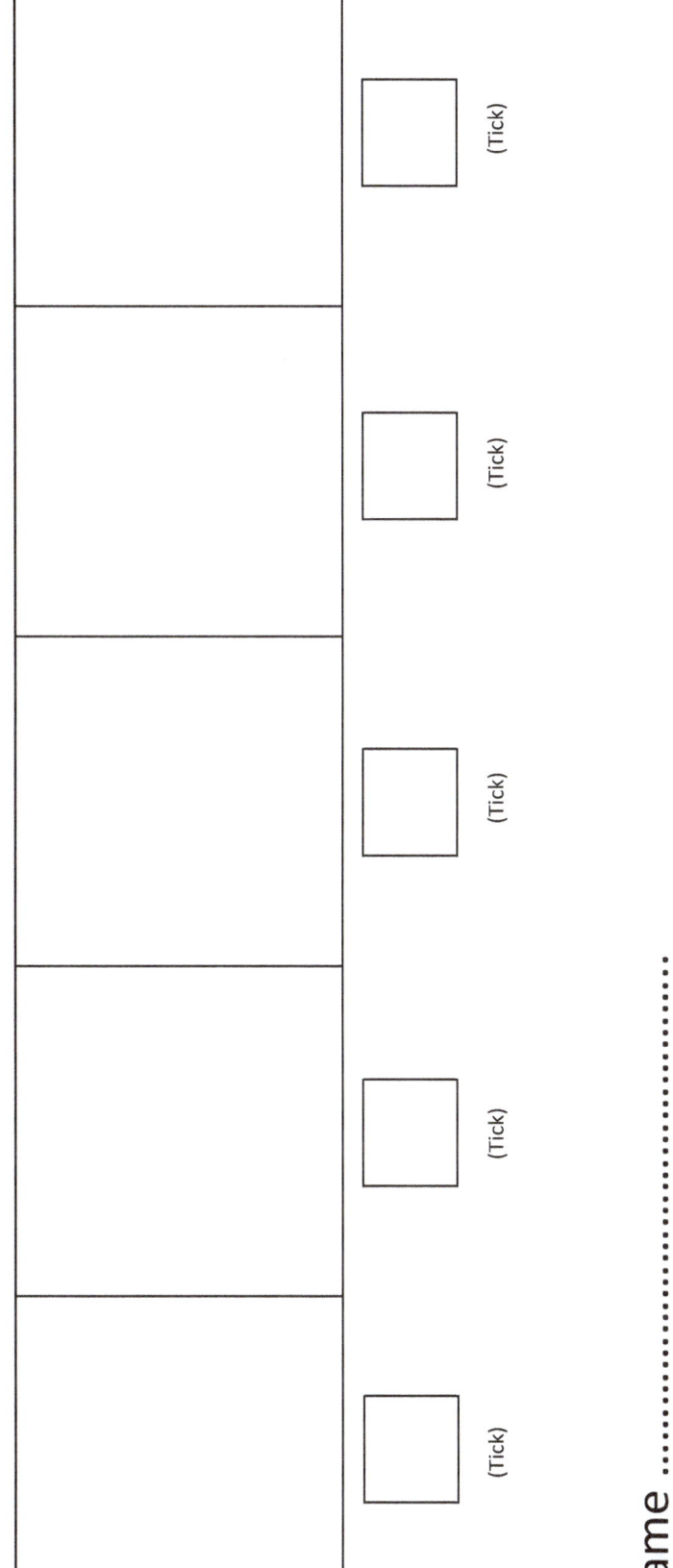

(Tick)	(Tick)	(Tick)	(Tick)	(Tick)

Name ....

Cut out the cards you need and add to the routine sheet.

Going to the Supermarket

Everyone needs to buy food to eat at home. This food is bought from shops.

Lots of people buy their food from a supermarket which is a really big shop.

Because it is so big, it can have lots of people in it and it can sometimes be noisy.

This can make me feel worried or anxious. It is okay to feel like this.

My adult will tell me when we are going and how long we will be in there for.

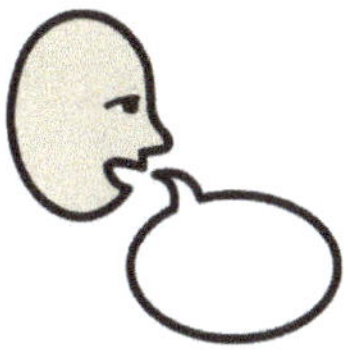

If I feel overwhelmed, I can tell my adult and we can take a break in a quieter area.

My adults will be happy when I can go to the supermarket with them.

I will feel happy too.

Mealtimes

Most meals are eaten at a table. At school I eat at a table and at home I eat at the table.

My adults at home will tell me if I need to sit at the table to eat my meal.

When I sit at the table, I will try hard to stay there until I have finished eating.

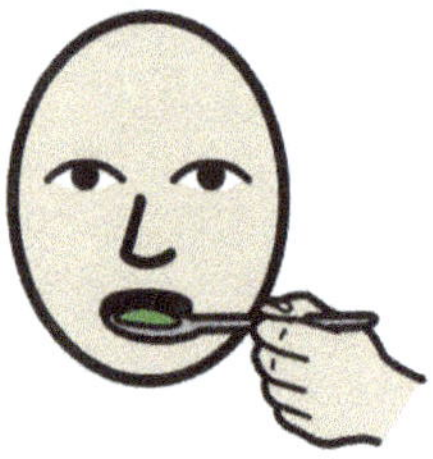

I might feel upset and I may not be able to sit really still. This is okay. I can tell my adults if I feel like this.

To help me, my adults will tell me what I will do next. They will say,

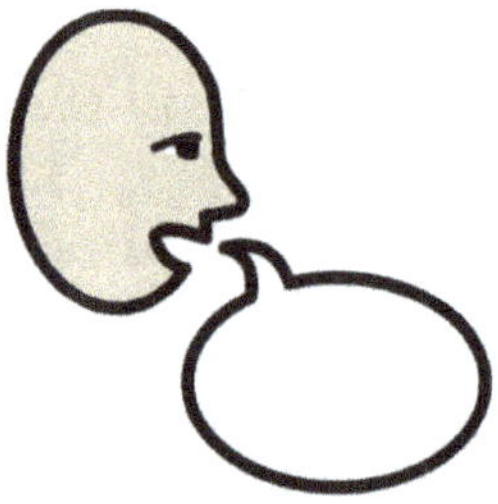

'First eat at the table, then ____________'.

My adults will be happy when I sit at the table to eat.

I will feel happy too.

Sleeping in My Own Bed

During the day, I can spend time with my family. This is 'family time' and my adults will tell me when this is.

Sometimes my family need to have time on their own. One of these times is at bedtime.
I will try really hard to stay in my bed, even if I am awake.

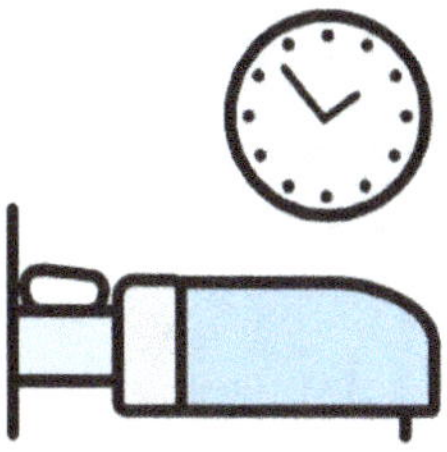

If I go to my adult, they will bring me back, wait 2 minutes and then go back to bed.
If I do not go into my adult's room and stay in my bed all night, I will get a smiley face on my reward chart.

I can go to my adult's room if there is an emergency.

I may feel upset about this at first. It is okay to feel like this and I will talk to my adult about it during the day.

My family will feel happy if I stay in my bed all night because we can all get a good night's sleep.

Reward Chart

☐	☐	☐	☐	☐

Monday	Tuesday	Wednesday	Thursday	Friday	Saturday	Sunday

(Tick)

My reward for 5 ticks is ....

My reward for 7 ticks is ....

Economy of Language

Information for Families

When speaking to your child at home, it can be easy to fall into the trap of 'over' explaining things when what is needed, is to use *less* language and give extra time for your child to process the information.

Please see below for some examples of this:

Instead of saying ...	Say ...
'We have a busy morning today. We need to get up because we are then going to the shop to buy some food for the family who are coming at ...'	'First get up, then we are going to the shops.' *(pause)* 'The family are coming over after that.' *(pause)*
'No, we can't have pizza again for tea tonight because we had it last week. We can't have pizza every week because it costs a lot of money to get a takeaway but also it is not healthy to have pizza all the time and ...'	'No, we are having chicken salad tonight.' *(pause)* 'It is healthier.' *(pause)*
'I don't want to be spoken to like that. I am your parent and it is rude to speak to me like that. I am not having you shout at me and not showing any respect because ...	'I don't like you speaking like that to me.' *(pause)* 'It is not respectful.' *(pause)*
'Can you pop upstairs for me and get my slippers please. I am pretty sure that I left them in the bottom of my wardrobe on the left-hand side. If they are not there, it may be worth looking by the side of my bed because ...'	'Can you get my slippers? They are in the wardrobe.' *(pause)* 'Or by my bed.' *(pause)*

Using Less Language

Sometimes adults use a lot of words when they don’t really need to. They do this because they think they are giving me lots of useful information.

When adults use all of these words, I can find it hard to follow what they are saying. This can mean that I don’t know what they have said and can make me feel overwhelmed. This is okay.

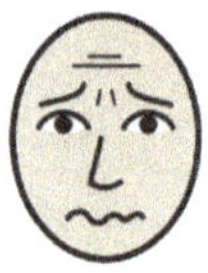

If I feel like this, I can say to my adult,

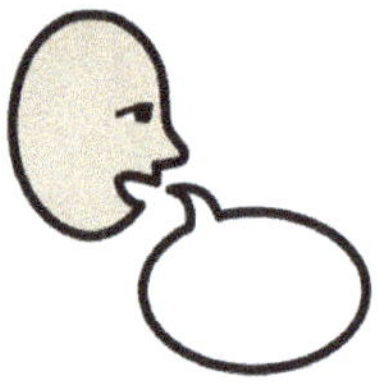

‘Can you please use less words to explain it to me?’

Adults can also speak very quickly. I can sometimes miss things that they say.

If this happens, I can say to my adult,

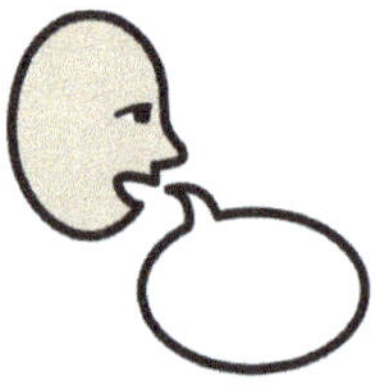

‘Can you please speak slower?’

If I say this to my adult, they will understand that I am finding the conversation difficult. They will use less words in their explanations and will speak slower.

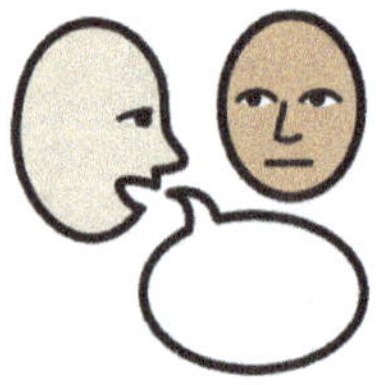

They will also give me more time to process what they have said.

IfI tell my adult when I feel like this, they will feel happy.I will feel happy too.

Chapter 3

Vocabulary Development

What Does this Chapter Cover?

- The importance of vocabulary
- Vocabulary exploration and development
- Discussions and good talk
- Emotional development and regulation

What Is Included in the Resources Section?

- Example of how to use the 'Word of the Week' in different contexts in school
- Vocabulary exploration sheet
- 'Word of the Week' sheet for families and an example
- Reading Talk Stems for families
- Restorative Conversation Talk Stems
- Restorative Conversation sheet
- Visual Feelings sheet
- 'One Page Profile' sheet and an example

The Importance of Vocabulary

To access learning, children need words (Branagan and Parsons, 2021, p. 3). A significant amount of learning relies on the use of language and for many children much of this language is implicitly 'picked up' throughout their school journey.

'Working memory is especially important to the formation of new words during the early stages of language acquisition' (Archibald, 2017, p. 6) and as children with Developmental Language Disorder often have a poor working memory, they can find learning new vocabulary a challenge. 'Late talkers' are likely to 'catch up' with their peers but children who have language difficulties which persist beyond 5½ years old should be considered for a diagnosis of DLD (Sowerbutts and Finer, 2019, p. 4).

DOI: 10.4324/9781032717869-3

As children with DLD struggle to pick up language incidentally, they require vocabulary to be explicitly taught. In fact, some writers believe that 'a limited response to language learning opportunities is, in effect, a diagnostic sign of DLD' (Bishop et al., 2016, cited in McGregor et al., 2021, pp. 22–23). To develop in this area, these children need to actually *hear* the words more times before they learn them and need to be explicitly shown how to use them. With relatively small changes to how vocabulary is taught, these children can learn new words too (Branagan and Parsons, 2021).

It has been documented that language ability (particularly vocabulary) plays a vital role in educational achievement (Spencer et al., 2017) and continues to impact right through life. One study found that children with poor vocabulary at five years of age had worse outcomes than typically developing peers at 34 years across a range of measures including education, employment and mental health (Law et al, 2009, cited in Parsons and Branagan, 2021, p. 2). Therefore, it is vital that schools prioritise vocabulary development to ensure the highest outcomes for all children and in particular, those with DLD.

This vocabulary is often categorised into three tiers:

- **Tier 1** are the basic words which typically appear in conversations and do not generally require explicit teaching but instead are implicitly learnt as children go through life, e.g. dog, warm, happy, apple, etc.
- **Tier 2** words are common but more complex. They are used in a variety of domains as the children progress through school, e.g. compare, precede, suggest, summarise, etc. As these words are characteristic of written text and rarely used in conversation, children are less likely to learn these words independently.
- **Tier 3** words are often referred to as 'topic words'. These words are rarely used and although they are required to be explicitly taught during the topic, it is unlikely that the child will be required to recall them again until the topic is revisited, e.g. conductor, precipitation, photosynthesis and biomes.

It is recommended that schools focus learning on the tier 2 level; it is regarded as the most productive approach (Beck, McKeown and Kucan, 2013) as they are the words that children are most 'likely to come across in a variety of contexts across the curriculum' (Bilton and Duff, 2021, p. 16). They are also the types of words which are frequently used in assessment questions. Often children are able to answer questions once they have been 're-phrased', proving that when a child gives an incorrect answer, it doesn't necessarily mean that they don't know the answer but rather that they didn't understand the question.

For example: in the question '*What impressions of the city do you get from these two paragraphs?*', if the child does not know what the words *impressions* and *paragraphs* means, they are unlikely to be able to answer this question. Whereas if the question was re-framed to '*What does this part tell you about the city?*', they may be able to give the answer required.

Vocabulary Exploration and Development

Being able to understand the meaning of words and use them to talk about the world is a fundamental skill for all learners (Branagan and Parsons, 2021). A study in 2016 found that educational outcomes could be predicted from a very early measurement of language development (Bleses et al., 2016, p. 15) and therefore a focus on vocabulary development in schools is essential.

However, for some children this process is more challenging and children entering school with comparatively limited vocabulary can find the increasing demands of the curriculum and the volume of words they are required to know causes an insurmountable barrier which in turn can affect learning and self-image (Branagan and Parsons, 2021).

Vocabulary teaching in schools tends to comprise of dictionary definitions whereas an approach where vocabulary meanings are directly explained along with thought-provoking, playful and interactive follow-up can be significantly more beneficial (Beck, McKeown and Kucan, 2013). The EEF (Education Endowment Foundation) recommend that the explicit teaching of new vocabulary should not be seen as an isolated activity but instead teachers should focus on providing students with repeated exposure to new vocabulary including modelling and scaffolding of its use to develop understanding and to show how new words can be used in a variety of contexts (Bilton and Duff, 2021). Children learn best when new words are heard in real sentences and are in a context that the child is familiar with (Parsons and Branagan, 2021).

Vocabulary development is vital and no matter how effective, one teacher in one year, or a short, focused intervention cannot make a difference and instead what is required is a sustained day-on-day, year-on-year, whole school approach (Parsons and Branagan, 2021). 'Enriching the word learning environment is not about one major change, but rather about creating a culture in which practitioners are able to reflect and make small changes that suit the children in their classes' (Parsons and Branagan, 2021, p. 28).

Below are some universal ideas to develop vocabulary:

- **Develop a vocabulary-rich environment:** This involves creating a culture in the classroom where learning new vocabulary is exciting, where new words are discovered and explored, where children feel happy and safe to ask what words mean and to experiment with new vocabulary in their learning. Word walls can be created, celebrated and regularly referred to not only during learning tasks but in the day-to-day language used in the classroom.
- **Word of the week:** A lot of schools will already have something similar to this in place. However, simply having it displayed in the classroom will not be enough for the words to be retained, particularly by those who find word learning a challenge. Instead, children need to hear the words in familiar contexts throughout a variety of situations, for example within instructions, during lessons, in the dinner hall and at home. As children hear the words in this variety of contexts, 'they will add new information and develop a richer and more complete understanding' (Parsons and Branagan, 2021, p. 7).
- **Vocabulary games:** For children to be excited about words and language, the adults around them need to be. There are lots of games that can be incorporated into the day and enjoyed by both the adults and the children. These games can be played at any time during the day when there are a few spare minutes, for example just before break time, at home time or within lessons.

For example:

  - **I spy** – this game needs no preparation. One player spots an item and says, 'I spy with my little eye, something beginning with <the letter>' and everyone else tries to guess.
  - **Charades** – words can be acted out by playing charades for others to guess from the actions without speaking. Focus words can be kept in a tub in the classroom and pulled out at random to play this game. Alternatively, this game can be played as part of a lesson based on the topic, for example in a grammar lesson, verbs could be acted out or in a geography lesson about the rainforest, the animals who live in the rainforest could be acted out.
  - **'I'm thinking of a word'** – again, this word could be picked out of the tub or focus on a particular topic. For this game, the person thinking of the word

gives clues for the class to guess. For example, in a grammar lesson which is exploring nouns, the clues could include: 'it is smaller than a television', 'it can be found in a fruit bowl', 'it is the same colour as a lemon', and so on.

- **20 questions** – similar to the game above, the word can be picked from a container or used as part of the lesson. However, this time, the class ask questions to which the person with the word can only say yes or no. For example, in a Personal, Social, Health and Economic (PSHE) lesson exploring emotions, the questions could include, 'Would I feel this when it is my birthday?', 'It is another word for happy?' and 'Does the word start with an "e"?' and so on.
- **Synonym game** – this involves choosing a word to explore synonyms, for example said, big, went. Two players stand up and the word is revealed. The players then take turns to say words that mean the same or similar to the word. For example, for the word 'said', they could say words such as 'bellowed, whispered, yelled, screamed'. The winner is the person who last says a word and their opponent cannot think of another (or if they repeat a word already said).
- **Category game** – this is the same game as the synonym game but rather than synonyms, this game focuses on words within categories, for example chocolate bars, ice-cream flavours, animals, sports, vehicles, fruits.

- **Language across the curriculum:** It is universally accepted that vocabulary is discussed, developed and taught with English lessons or heavy language-based lessons such as geography or history, but how often is vocabulary explored in art or PE? Having a vocabulary focus in *all* lessons across the curriculum is beneficial for all children.
- **Spotlight sessions:** This involves shining a 'spotlight' on one paragraph and then exploring the tier 2 vocabulary within in it. The class reads the paragraph first, then the tier 2 vocabulary is explored through the use of visuals and photographs and by putting the words in a context that the children will understand. The paragraph is then read for a second time, allowing the children to have a deeper understanding of the content.

For example, look at the short paragraph below aimed at Year 5/6 students:

*Although sometimes considered the inventor of the **steam engine** which used **coal** as **fuel, James Watt** in fact did NOT invent it, but did make great improvements to it by*

> *making it more efficient. Prior to this, machines relied on **waterpower** which meant they must be built near water. The invention of the **steam engine** allowed **factories** to be built anywhere in the country.*

In bold are the tier 3 'topic words' related to the Industrial Revolution which are important in terms of learning about the topic. However, it is the green tier 2 words that are an imperative factor as to whether the child understands what they are reading or not.

Targeted/ Specialist Strategies

In schools, educators are well aware of the importance of developing their students' vocabulary, and where students are identified as struggling in this area, out-of-class interventions are often put in place. While well-intentioned, these interventions can have little impact as the focus words are often not heard enough times outside the group or in the classroom to be fully established and the children who struggle with language can find it a challenge to generalise to other contexts (Branagan and Parsons, 2021). A study in 2023, in contrast to previous studies, and aligned with inclusive education policy, identified an agreement 'between teachers and children on the many practical classroom strategies that can support the inclusion of the child with DLD in the classroom' (Gibbons, Coughlan and Gallagher, 2023, p. 9).

For greater impact for all students, and to promote inclusivity for those children with DLD or who struggle with language, the focus should remain on whole-class teaching, making small adaptations as necessary as 'small changes, when done regularly as part of standard teaching, will go a long way to supporting vulnerable word learners' (Branagan and Parsons, 2021, p. 14).

As well as the whole-class activities listed above, below are some of the 'adaptations' that can be made on a targeted/ specialist level:

- **Being aware of the students' starting points:** It is important to have high expectations of all children. However, to ensure that any children who struggle with language or who have DLD do not become overwhelmed or disengaged from the learning, it is also important that educators are aware of the level of language that the children understand rather than *assuming* what they know based on their age. This way, these children can be supported to progress from their individual starting points.

- **Vocabulary books and exploration time:** Children could be encouraged to record any words that they come across during the day that they don't understand which can then be explored either in school or taken home to look at with families. It could be that a 'vocabulary exploration time' is timetabled at the end of each day where dictionaries are out on the tables and the teacher can focus in on groups or individuals for more targeted support.
- **Individual, personalised dictionaries:** This involves children having a personal dictionary in which they record new words they have learnt and/or words that they find tricky. For the greatest impact, the words should be recorded alongside a visual and there should be some exploration of meaning and how to put it in a sentence in context. An example of a vocabulary exploration sheet can be found at the end of this chapter. The 'Word Wizard' sheet from the Word Aware series would also be perfect for this (Parsons and Branagan, 2021, p. 207).
- **Tier 2 vocabulary interventions:** Although language development within the whole-class setting has the most impact, an out-of-class intervention that has a curriculum focus has a number of advantages: these words are likely to be used more frequently in the classroom, children will be more able to engage with the content in lessons and their peers will also be learning the same words, all of which can boost self-esteem and confidence (Branagan and Parsons, 2021). An example of a tier 2 vocabulary intervention which would benefit children who struggle with language would be to explore the words used in the SAT style assessment questions – words such as compare, imply, impression, describe, infer, and so on.

  For more ideas and information about teaching small group vocabulary interventions, see: Word Aware 3: Teaching Vocabulary in Small Groups for Ages 6 to 11 (Branagan and Parsons, 2021).

Parents, Carers and Families

Vocabulary reflects all aspects of learning and life experiences, and to be really embedded, needs to be heard multiple times in different contexts. Therefore, it makes sense to build a team of people who work with or know these children who can work together to provide optimal word learning opportunities (Branagan and Parsons, 2021). The home environment can have a significant effect on a child's vocabulary and therefore it is beneficial to ensure that parents, carers and families (a) understand the importance of developing vocabulary and (b) know *how* they can support their child's vocabulary at home.

Below are some ways that this can be done:

- Vocabulary sheets for families to explore with their child at home
- Information about activities and games they can play at home based on focus vocabulary. For example:
    - Focus activities for families to do at home with their child, e.g. count the syllables, say the sounds, identify rhyming words, find the meaning, synonyms, antonyms etc.
    - Challenges – how many times can you use the word <focus word> at home this weekend?
- Involve the parent in the development and use of focus words, for example, sending home an information sheet about how these words could be used at home in different situations, for example at meal times, bedtime or at the park.

Examples of how word of the week can be used in school in different contexts, for families at home (including a blank format) and the vocabulary exploration sheet, can be found in the resources section at the end of this chapter.

Reflection: *Consider your setting and how much inclusive, universal support could be given in place of weekly, out-of-the-classroom interventions. Consider how you could develop 'teams' around the child to support vocabulary development.*

Discussions and Good Talk

For all children, 'speaking and listening are at the heart of all language development. They are foundational for reading and writing, while proving essential for thinking and communication' (Bilton and Duff, 2021, p. 13), but for children with DLD, this is even more so. Below are strategies for all students to compliment high quality teaching and to further develop children's expressive language.

- **Encourage children to speak in full sentences:** Language is learnt best by repeatedly exposing children to new vocabulary. This includes modelling, scaffolding and developing a deeper understanding for children by hearing this vocabulary across a variety of contexts (Bilton and Duff, 2021) and in real sentences that are familiar to the child (Parsons and Branagan, 2021).

  Encouraging children to speak in full sentences supports them to organise their thoughts and to formulate responses, to practice a variety of grammar and language structures and to use learnt vocabulary correctly in context, all of which support good writing skills.

- **Talk stems:** These are sentence starters that are used to support children to orally formulate sentences. For example, *'The character feels hopeless because …', 'The reason that the light turned on was …' or 'I know that the answer is 245 because …'*, and so on. They can be used effectively during whole-class teaching, group work and partner work. They can be created at the time and written on the board, added to the lesson PowerPoint or printed out and put on the table for group or partner work.
- **Talk activities:** Classroom talk is vital as part of the learning process. The EEF state that 'Approaches that promote talk and interaction between learners tend to result in the best gains' (Bilton and Duff, 2021, p. 14), and although it is common for teachers to include talk activities as part of English lessons, it is beneficial for these talk-based activities to be in every lesson. For example, below are some examples of talk stems used in a Year 3 history lesson about the Stone Age, focusing on coordinating conjunctions:

- They used animal skins to make clothes **for** …
- They didn't have food shops **yet** …
- During the Stone Age, people ate meat **and** …
- They didn't have knives and forks **nor** did they have …
- It was very cold **but** …

Targeted/Specialist Strategies

Any of the universal strategies for developing good talk can be adapted for groups or individuals as needed. For example:

Group/individual talk stems: Talk stems can also be used for a group or on an individual basis to develop more focused vocabulary. For example, in a science lesson, where children are discussing the results of an experiment, it may be that a group of children in class need to practice the conjunction 'because' so talk stems can be provided to structure these sentences, for example. The red car went faster because …, The blue car didn't go as fast because …, The cars went faster on the plastic surface because … etc.

Developing individual good talk: During lessons, it may be beneficial for a group/ individuals to practice orally formulating sentences more than others (e.g. a child with DLD), therefore it may be useful to develop this on a group and/or individual basis. This may be through the use of talk partners, a small group, adult-led discussion or on a 1:1 basis with an adult.

Parents, Carers and Families

Talk stems: Promoting good talk at home can be significantly beneficial for all children. The adult-child interactions that take place during shared reading are thought to be the key ingredient to their success (Poortvliet, Axford and Lloyd, 2018, p. 13). For young children, promoting shared reading should be a central component of working with families as a way of supporting oral language development and early literacy (Poortvliet, Axford and Lloyd, 2018, p. 13). As children get older ... engaging in high quality talk about the story remains important for fostering reading comprehension skills (Poortvliet, Axford and Lloyd, 2018, p. 14).

Sending home talk stems for families to use when reading with their child can support high quality discussions. An example of how this could be done can be found in the resources section at the end of this chapter.

Reflection: *Think about how discussion and good talk are promoted and supported in your setting. Do you regularly use talk partner activities? Are the children encouraged to speak in full sentences and explicitly taught how to have discussions using talk stems?*

Emotional Development and Regulation

In 2007 a study was completed that found that language difficulties impacted on children's literacy development and so put them at greater risk of social, emotional and behavioural difficulties at school (Lindsay, Dockrell and Strand, 2007, p. 15). Children with DLD can often be misunderstood and, at times, the behaviours that they display can be misinterpreted as negative behaviour. Because of this, they can be more prone to demonstrating a social, emotional and/or mental health need. It is therefore vital that schools recognise this and support social and emotional wellbeing as well as academic success at school.

Below are some of the areas of difficulty that children with DLD can have which can be misunderstood or misinterpreted by adults both in school and at home:

- **Holding information in their heads:** Struggling to hold information in their heads can mean children with DLD can find it a challenge to follow more than one instruction at a time.

  This can be interpreted by adults to be the child *choosing* to ignore the instruction or not listening to the teacher.

- **Retaining information**: Children with DLD can struggle to retain information and therefore can struggle to remember information from one lesson to the next (or even within one lesson).

  This can be interpreted by adults that the child hasn't been listening in the lessons.

- **Social interaction**: Children with DLD can misunderstand or misinterpret rules of games in the playground and can unintentionally sound disrespectful due to a lack of understanding around social rules and cues.

  This can be interpreted as them being unkind to other children and disrespectful to adults. As a result of this, they can not only be told off by adults but can also find that other children do not want to play with them.

- **Sentence formulation**: Children with DLD find it difficult to formulate sentences and express their feelings and therefore if there has been an argument, they can struggle to explain what happened, how they feel or articulate that they didn't understand.

  This can mean that adults dealing with the fall out can think that they are to blame and give them a consequence.

- **Focus and attention**: Children with DLD can find focus and attention a challenge.

  This can lead the adult to believe that they are not concentrating or trying hard in the lesson.

Children with DLD can be trying really hard in class but often adults can misinterpret their behaviour as laziness or assume that they are not trying hard which can be very frustrating for the child. With at least 60% of young people accessing youth justice services in the UK having speech, language and communication needs (Bryan et al., 2015, p. 2), it is essential that language difficulties are identified as early as possible in schools and that those children experiencing educational or emotional difficulties are routinely assessed for speech, language and communication difficulties (Bryan et al., 2015, p. 1).

For any children displaying social, emotional and mental health difficulties including behavioural difficulties, the following strategies can be used to support these students to have a better understanding of their emotions and feelings, to develop a knowledge of strategies to help them to regulate and to support them to communicate to others at these times so a better understanding of the child can be gained.

Zones of Regulation:

This is a 'conceptual framework used to teach students self-regulation' (Kuypers, 2011, p. 8) which categorises feelings into four coloured zones – blue, green, yellow and red. It supports children to become familiar with each state using common language and promoting strategies to support transitioning back into the 'green' zone (happy, focused, content, calm and proud), the optimal place to be to learn.

Whole-class activities based on this programme can include:

- Having a Zones of Regulation poster on the wall for all children to put their names on in a morning so adults can easily and immediately see any children who need support first thing in the morning.
- The four colours can be on tables so children can write their names on the corresponding colour to reflect how they are feeling and move it as and when needed.
- Classes can have four coloured boxes or small buckets that correspond to the four coloured zones. Children can then put their names in these in a morning but move them if needed, for example after break time or lunchtime. This way, adults can easily see if there is anyone in the class needing support.
- These four zones can be referred to as part of lessons throughout the day, for example when looking at stories or events in English lessons, reading sessions or foundation subjects such as History or RE and refer to the 'Zone' that different people or characters may be in and why.
- The zones can be linked to any common themes arising within the class. For younger children, a puppet could be used to cover some of the situations that have happened through discussion of which zone the puppet is in, why they are in it and what they can do to return to the green zone. For older children, the same can be done through scenarios based on real-life incidents that have happened in school.

Narrating emotions:

Whenever emotions are seen in school, it is useful to narrate these feelings and emotions. This can be linked to the Zones of Regulation if the school uses this programme, but it is not essential. See below for some examples:

Situation	Adult response
A child is worried about an activity in class.	'I can see that you are feeling worried. Shall I come and talk you through the activity?'
A child is angry at playtime.	'I can see you are angry. Shall we go inside and find a strategy to help you to feel calmer?'
A child is upset in the dinner hall because of a fall out with a friend.	'I can see you are upset. Would you like to tell me about it?'
A child comes to school excited about getting a badge at Brownies.	'I can see you are very excited. Would you like to tell the class about your exciting news?'
A child is happy because they have just got 10/10 in a maths test.	'I can tell you are really happy with your score. You have worked really hard and should be very proud of yourself.'

For the greatest impact, this vocabulary should be introduced and regularly referred to from the early years. For younger children it is useful to stick to the basic emotions to start with (happy, sad, excited and angry) and to use visuals to accompany these feelings which all adults can wear on lanyards, so they are easily accessible.

Once children become familiar with naming their emotions, they can begin to describe their physical symptoms when they feel the emotion. See below for how the scripts above can be developed in each example:

Situation	Adult response
A child is worried about an activity in class.	'I can see that you are feeling worried. Shall I come and talk you through the activity?' When I feel worried, my tummy sometimes hurts or I can get a headache – how are you feeling?'
A child is angry at playtime.	'I can see you are angry. Shall we go inside and find a strategy to help you to feel calmer?' When I feel angry, it can make me feel like I have a fire in my tummy, or it can make me want to cry – how are you feeling?'

Situation	Adult response
A child is upset in the dinner hall because of a fallout with a friend.	'I can see you are upset. Would you like to tell me about it?' When I feel upset, it can make me feel like crying or sometimes shouting and I can feel like I don't want to talk to anyone – how are you feeling?'
A child comes to school excited about getting a badge at Brownies.	'I can see you are very excited. Would you like to tell the class about your exciting news?' When I feel excited, I can feel very giddy inside and I can find it hard to sit still – is that how you are feeling?'
A child is happy because they have just got 10/10 in a maths test.	'I can tell you are really happy with your score. You have worked really hard and should be very proud of yourself.' When I feel happy, my insides can feel warm, and I have a big smile on my face – can you describe how you are feeling?'

Regulation stations:

Being able to name emotions and know that they affect you physically is important for children to know. Once they can do this, then they can develop strategies to regulate if they are feeling strong emotions. This doesn't always have to be anger or upset but can include being very excitable. When children need a strategy, one idea is for classes to have 'Regulation stations' which could have items on for each emotion.

See below for ideas for the regulation station:

- Coloured boxes (or boxes labelled with the emotion) could have items in them to support regulation, for example, fidget toys, colouring sheets and visual cards for deep breathing. Children could choose an item and a five-minute timer and take it to their table.
- Laminated cards with strategies on could be provided for each emotion and children could collect a card and either do the activities at the station or at their tables. For example, counting activities, breathing cards or grounding techniques and so on.
- The regulation station could be a table that a child sits at or an area to go to in the classroom which has a poster of the emotions and then strategies attached with Velcro which the children can choose to use in the area for five minutes.

Restorative conversations:

If children have fallen out or if there has been an incident at school, restorative conversations afterwards are vital to give children the opportunity to communicate their feelings as well as hearing and considering feelings from the other person's point of view. Adults can facilitate this conversation by modelling how to take turns and how to respond to the other child. Time should be given to these conversations to ensure that both children feel listened to, feel that they have been able to express their views and to be able to resolve the situation. It is also hoped that if these conversations are carried out regularly that (a) incidents would become less frequent as children may start to see things from other people's point of view and (b) where they do happen, children may begin to have these conversations independently.

Talk stems are useful to use in these situations. This could be as simple as a laminated card which the children can access, and which include talk stems such as,

'I felt ______ today because ____________', 'I felt _____ when ____________',

'I didn't like it when ____________' and 'I'm sorry if you felt __________'.

Visuals can also be added to these so all children can access them.

Targeted/Specialist Strategies

Below are some strategies to help children who require a more targeted/specialist level of support to manage their emotional developmental and regulation:

- **Group/individual use of the Zones of Regulation:** If there are children who are struggling with their emotions and require extra, targeted input, the Zones of Regulation curriculum can be used for both small group or 1:1 work. There are lots of activities in the book, *The Zones of Regulation: a curriculum designed to foster self-regulation and emotional control* by Leah M. Kuypers (2011).
- **One page profiles:** For children with DLD and/or those students who struggle to manage their emotions, consistency is key. For most children in primary schools, class teachers are with their class for the majority of the week. However, there are inevitably times when other adults are in class. For example, during Planning, Preparation and Assessment (PPA) time or if the teacher is absent for school. In secondary schools, students encounter a wider variety of staff so

ensuring consistency across all members of staff for these students is even more important.

'One Page Profiles' detail information such as the student's strengths and things that they like, things that they find difficult, how best to communicate with them, triggers for the child and strategies that work for them when dis-regulated (and ones that definitely don't!). These profiles can ensure that *all* adults are consistent for the child and know how best to support them.

Where possible, it can be beneficial to create these profiles *with* the student and make them in a child friendly format including visuals. To begin with, adults can support the child to refer to this when they need to use a strategy, but over time, they can be taught to use this independently by checking how they are feeling and selecting a strategy that will help them.

- **Calm bags/boxes:** These are a collection of items that support the child to regulate and are bespoke to the individual. Examples of items that could be in here include colouring sheets, soft toys, fidget toys, sprays, hand creams, ear defenders and so on. These can work alongside the One Page Profile (OPP) which can include photographs of the items that are in the calm bag/box. For example, if a child has come in after break feeling slightly agitated or over-excitable and struggling to settle and focus, they could refer to their OPP, see what item is linked to this emotion and then choose that out of the box (e.g. a colouring sheet).

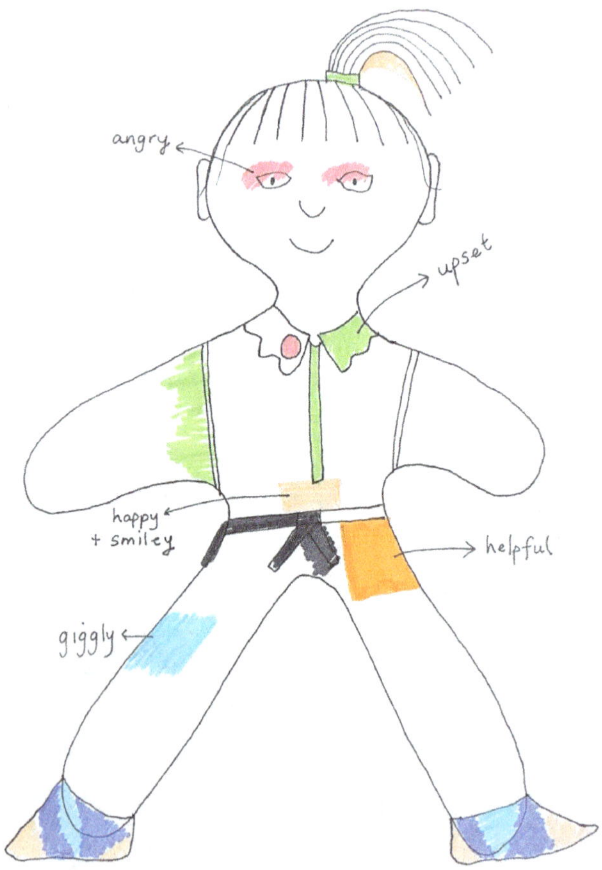

FIGURE 3.1

- **Parts picture:** Children with DLD (and those who struggle with their emotions) can find it a challenge to view themselves positively and instead can believe that the negative part of themselves (e.g. anger) is solely who they are. The process of completing a parts picture involves the adult encouraging the child to think of both the 'positive' and 'negative' aspects of themselves (Bomber, 2007), finding evidence of these parts and recording them on an outline of a body (either printed or drawn by either the adult or the child).

When recording the 'part' on the picture, it can be interesting to ask the child where they want to put this part on their body or to draw an arrow to where they feel this part. Doing this can give an interesting insight into how children feel when they are experiencing different emotions and sometimes why they react in the way that they do. For example, if they feel anger in their eyes, this is useful information as adults will probably be able to tell by looking at this child that they are angry. Alternatively, if they label anger in their hands/fists or mouth, this can explain why they lash out physically or verbally when angry.

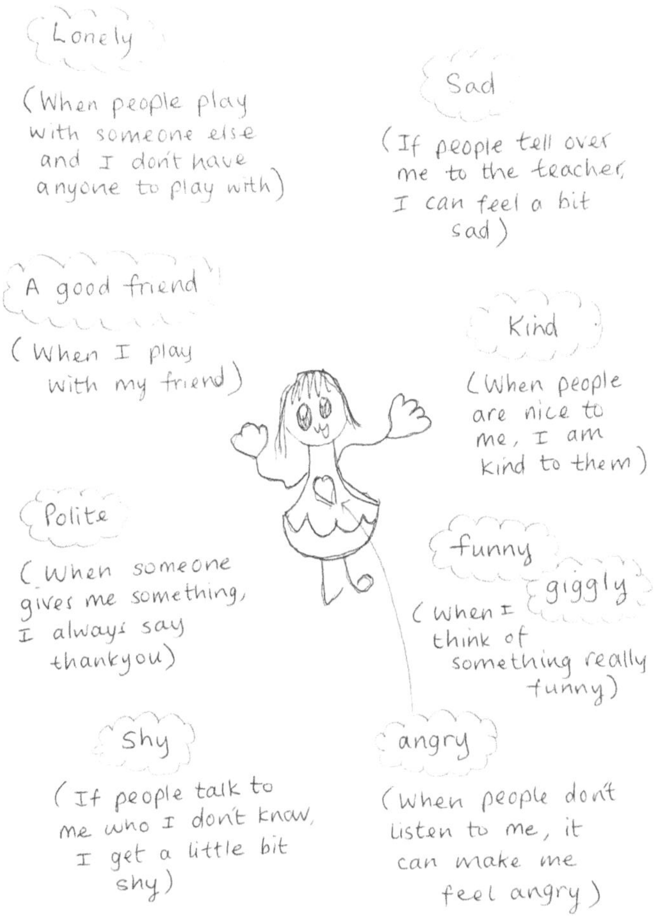

FIGURE 3.2

- This can be started and then added to over time as more 'parts' are noticed and can then become part of the vocabulary with this child (e.g. *'I have just seen your polite part because I saw you hold the door open for our visitor'* or *'I saw your proud part just then when you received your certificate in assembly'*). It can also be beneficial to use this language during times of dysregulation or during restorative conversations (e.g. *'I can see that your angry part is very cross'* or *'Your impatient part seemed to take over when you pushed in the line'*).

Doing this allows the child to see all the parts that make them who they are, all the positive parts they have and to realise that any aspects that they find difficult do not define them.

- **Talk stems and templates for regulation and restoration:** Because children with DLD find it difficult to hold information in their heads and to formulate sentences, it is even more vital to provide them with methods of recording their feelings and to communicate these to adults during times of dysregulation as well as during restorative conversations.

  To support this, the following resources could be made available for any child who needs them:
  - Laminated cards or sheets of paper with feelings visuals on to take when needed and to simply circle or tick how they are feeling.
  - Talk stems alongside visuals to support them to tell an adult what has happened.
  - A sheet with visuals on which children can simply tick or circle and pass to an adult if needed.
  - Restoration talk stems to support the child to talk through the incident once everyone has regulated.
- **Talking mats:** Talking mats were first developed from a research project by Joan Murphy in 1998 at the University of Stirling. Murphy was studying the interactions of people with cerebral palsy and realised that they didn't have the vocabulary required so came up with the idea of a visual framework (talkingmats.com).

  These are now widely used in primary schools to gain pupil voice. They are not only useful for children who do not have the vocabulary but also children who struggle to articulate their thoughts and feelings. Children may find being asked direct questions such as 'Why are you feeling upset?' or 'What is making you feel angry?' difficult to answer. They may also not know what is making them feel that way. However, using a talking mat and sorting pictures such as 'maths', 'friends' or 'the classroom' into what is a 'Big problem', 'Little problem' and 'No problem' for them, can help the child to organise their thoughts and begin to elaborate on each picture. This then gives the adult an insight into why the child is feeling how they are and informs them of the necessary support to put in place.

Parents, Carers and Families

One page profiles – ensuring consistency across school *and* home is vital to support children so it can be helpful to share the One Page Profiles with families. Furthermore, as children can often demonstrate different behaviours at home than at school, adults at home may be able to contribute to these documents so involving them in the creation process would be beneficial for all.

Talking mats – These can be useful either for families to do at home with their child or for school to do and to share with home. For example, if the adult at home is struggling to get their child dressed in a morning, school could send home a talking mat with pictures to sort including the room, the different clothes, the adult, the instructions and so on, so they can find out what the child is finding difficult with a view to removing this barrier and enabling them to get dressed in a morning.

Children with DLD can find the school environment overwhelming which could eventually result in them thinking negatively about school and feeling like they don't want to attend. Using a talking mat for this can be a vital component in getting the child into school, removing any barriers for them and ensuring that they feel comfortable and happy to attend school.

An example of restorative talk stems, a restorative conversation sheet, a visual feelings record sheet and a One Page Profile (template and an example) can be found in the resources section at the end of this chapter.

Reflection: *Think about any children that you work with who seem to ignore instructions, who are seemingly unable to retain information, who struggle with friendships, focus and attention or emotional regulation. Review what you have in place to support these children and consider assessing these children for a speech, language and communication need.*

Key Takeaways from Chapter 3

- A significant amount of learning relies on the use of language, and it has been found that language ability (particularly vocabulary) plays a vital role in educational achievement. Therefore, it is essential that schools **prioritise vocabulary** development.
- Making **small adaptations** to how vocabulary is taught within the whole-class environment has a greater impact than weekly out-of-class interventions although there is a place for curriculum-based interventions.
- Developing a **vocabulary/ language rich environment** where learning and exploring new words is celebrated and time is given to ensuring that children have a deeper, embedded understanding of new vocabulary, is beneficial for all.
- **Speaking and listening are at the heart of all language development.**
- Children and young people with DLD struggle with learning new vocabulary incidentally and require new words **explicitly teaching** to them which involves exploring the word, the meaning, putting it in context and constant repetition.
- There are behaviours that children with DLD can present with which can easily be misinterpreted as negative behaviour and, therefore, educators must put processes in place to **ensure that these children can communicate their thoughts and feelings** and have strategies to support them to regulate when required.
- Many young people accessing youth justice services in the UK have speech, language and communication needs so it is **essential that language difficulties are identified as early as possible** and that those children experiencing educational or emotional difficulties are routinely assessed for a speech, language, and communication need.

References

Archibald, L.M. (2017). Working memory and language learning: A review. *Child Language Teaching and Therapy*, *33*(1), pp. 5–17.

Beck, I.L., McKeown, M.G. and Kucan, L. (2013). *Bringing Words to Life: Robust Vocabulary Instruction*. Guilford Press.

Bleses, D., Makransky, G., Dale, P.S., Højen, A. and Ari, B.A. (2016). Early productive vocabulary predicts academic achievement 10 years later. *Applied Psycholinguistics*, *37*(6), pp. 1461–1476.

Bomber, L.M. (2007). *Inside I'm Hurting: Practical Strategies for Supporting Children with Attachment Difficulties in Schools*. Worth.

Branagan, A. and Parsons, S. (2021). *Word Aware 3: Teaching Vocabulary in Small Groups for Ages 6 to 11*. Routledge.

Bryan, K., Garvani, G., Gregory, J. and Kilner, K. (2015). Language difficulties and criminal justice: The need for earlier identification. *International Journal of Language & Communication Disorders, 50*(6), pp. 763–775.

EEF (2021). Improving Literacy in Key Stage 2. Guidance Report. Education Endowment Foundation. Available at https://educationendowmentfoundation.org.uk/education-evidence/guidance-reports/literacy-ks2 [accessed 7 April 2024].

Gibbons, M., Coughlan, K. and Gallagher, A. (2023). Hidden in plain sight: A qualitative exploration of teachers and children's perspectives on supporting developmental language disorder in school. *Advances in Communication and Swallowing, 26*(1), pp. 3–12.

Kuypers, L.M. (2011). *The Zones of Regulation: A Curriculum Designed to Foster Self-regulation and Emotional Control*. Think Social Publishing, Inc.

Lindsay, G., Dockrell, J.E. and Strand, S. (2007). Longitudinal patterns of behaviour problems in children with specific speech and language difficulties: Child and contextual factors. *British Journal of Educational Psychology, 77*(4), pp. 811–828.

McGregor, K.K., Van Horne, A.O., Curran, M., Cook, S.W. and Cole, R. (2021). The challenge of rich vocabulary instruction for children with developmental language disorder. *Language, Speech, and Hearing Services in Schools, 52*(2), pp. 467–484.

Parsons, S. and Branagan, A. (2021). *Word Aware 1: Teaching Vocabulary Across the Day, Across the Curriculum*. Routledge.

Sowerbutts, A. and Finer, A. (2019). *DLD and Me: Supporting Children and Young People with Developmental Language Disorder*. Routledge.

Spencer, S., Clegg, J., Stackhouse, J. and Rush, R. (2017). Contribution of spoken language and socio-economic background to adolescents' educational achievement at age 16 years. *International Journal of Language & Communication Disorders, 52*(2), pp. 184–196.

Van Poortvliet, M., Axford, N. and Lloyd, J. (2018). Working with parents to support children's learning: guidance report. *Education Endowment Foundation.*

Recommended Books and Websites

Branagan, A. and Parsons, S. (2021). *Word Aware 3: Teaching Vocabulary in Small Groups for Ages 6 to 11*. Routledge.

Parsons, S. and Branagan, A. (2021). *Word Aware 1: Teaching Vocabulary Across the Day, Across the Curriculum*. Routledge.

Talking mats. Available at Our Story – Improving Communication, Improving Lives (talkingmats.com) [accessed 31 October 2024].

Zones of Regulation. Available at The Zones of Regulation | A Curriculum for Emotional Regulation [accessed 31 October 2024].

Chapter 3

Resources Section

Word of the Week

Using a focus word in different contexts

It is beneficial for children to hear newly taught vocabulary in familiar contexts and in a variety of ways to best support their understanding of the new word as well as their retention of this vocabulary.

Please see below for ways that this could be done.

Focus word: ***emphasise***

1. When giving instructions: *'I am going to* ***emphasise*** *the first instruction so you remember it.'*

2. When responding to answers: *'I would like to* ***emphasise*** *what <name> just said because it was a really important point.'*

3. When teaching phonics: *'Which sound in the word did I just* ***emphasise****?'*

4. In a history lesson: *'I am* ***emphasising*** *the importance of this event.'*

5. When going for dinner: *'I would like to* ***emphasise*** *the importance of walking when we go to the dinner hall so nobody gets hurt.'*

6. When sending children home: *'Could you please* ***emphasise*** *to your families how important it is for them to return the form?'*

7. In assembly: 'I am going to **emphasise** the words I am going to say when I would like you to clap along.'

To pass onto families to use at home:

1. I am going to **emphasise** what time is bedtime tonight, so you don't forget it.

2. I **emphasise** how important it is to give this envelope to your teacher.

3. I **emphasise** how dangerous it is to get too close to the fire.

Vocabulary Exploration

New Word ....

It starts with ....

It has .... syllables

It rhymes with ....

Act it out and find an action for this word.

Draw a picture or draw your action for this word here.

What word class is this word (e.g. noun, verb) ? ....

Does this word have more than one meaning? ....

Write the meanings below:

Meaning 1:.............................

....

Write it in a sentence:

....

....

Meaning 2:.............................

....

Write it in a sentence:

....

....

Meaning 3:.............................

....

Write it in a sentence:

....

....

Word of the Week

Parents, Carers and Families

This week, our word of the week in school is ....

Please see below for ways in which you could use this word at home to support your child's understanding and to encourage them to use this vocabulary in a variety of contexts.

- ☐
- ☐
- ☐
- ☐
- ☐

Word of the Week

Example for Parents, Carers and Families

This week, our word of the week in school is …*yearning*….

Please see below for ways in which you could use this word at home to support your child's understanding and to encourage them to use this vocabulary in a variety of contexts.

- ☐ At teatime: I am *yearning* for my dinner because I am so hungry.
- ☐ In the morning: I bet you are *yearning* to get outside and play in the fresh air.
- ☐ When watching TV together: I think this character is *yearning* to see their mum.
- ☐ At lunchtime: Dad is *yearning* for a sandwich.
- ☐ When playing with siblings: I think it is your brother's turn, he is *yearning* for a go!
- ☐ When meeting friends: Shall we set off, I am *yearning* to see them again.
- ☐ At bedtime: It is nearly bedtime, I am *yearning* for a good long sleep!
- ☐ When eating: Have you nearly finished your dinner, I am *yearning* for a piece of that cake.
- ☐ When reading together: Let's read one more chapter, I am *yearning* to know what happened to them next.

Reading Talk Stems

These talk stems can be used at home to initiate conversations, to develop your child's vocabulary and to support them with their reading.

Q: Can you point to a ..... on the page?

Yes, I can point to a ....

Q: Can you find something that....?

Yes, I can find ...

Q: What does ..... mean?

..... means ......

Q: Why do you think that person is...?

I think they are .... because....

Q: Can you think of a time when you have...?

Yes, I remember when ....

Q: How do they feel? How do you know?

I think they feel... because...

Q: Can you think of a time when you felt ...?

Yes, I remember feeling .... when ....

Restorative Talk Stems

I felt ______ because ...

I didn't like it when ...

I didn't understand ...

I was thinking ...

I thought that they were ...

Restorative Talk Stems

I felt ______ because ...

I didn't like it when ...

I didn't understand ...

I was thinking ...

I thought that they were ...

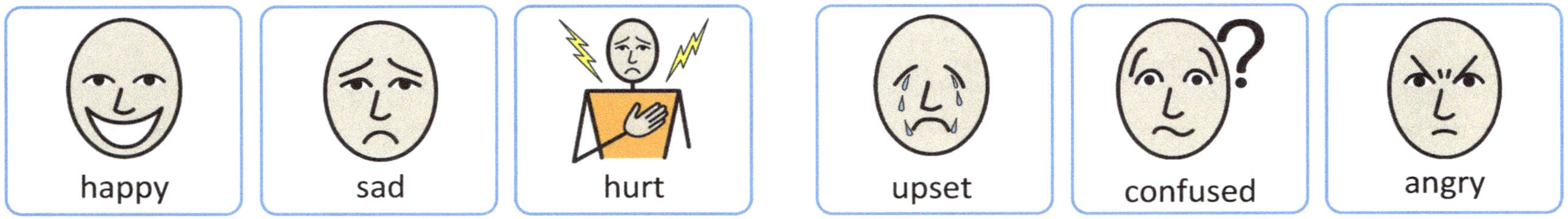

What happened?

I felt ______ today because
____________.
I didn't like it when __________.

How did you feel?

I felt ______ when
_________.
I feel ______.

Who else was involved? How do you think they felt?

_____ was involved.
I think they felt ___ because _________.

How can we make it better?

To make it better we could __________.

- Say sorry to each other
- Shake hands
- Write a sorry note
- Something else

How can we stop this from happening again?

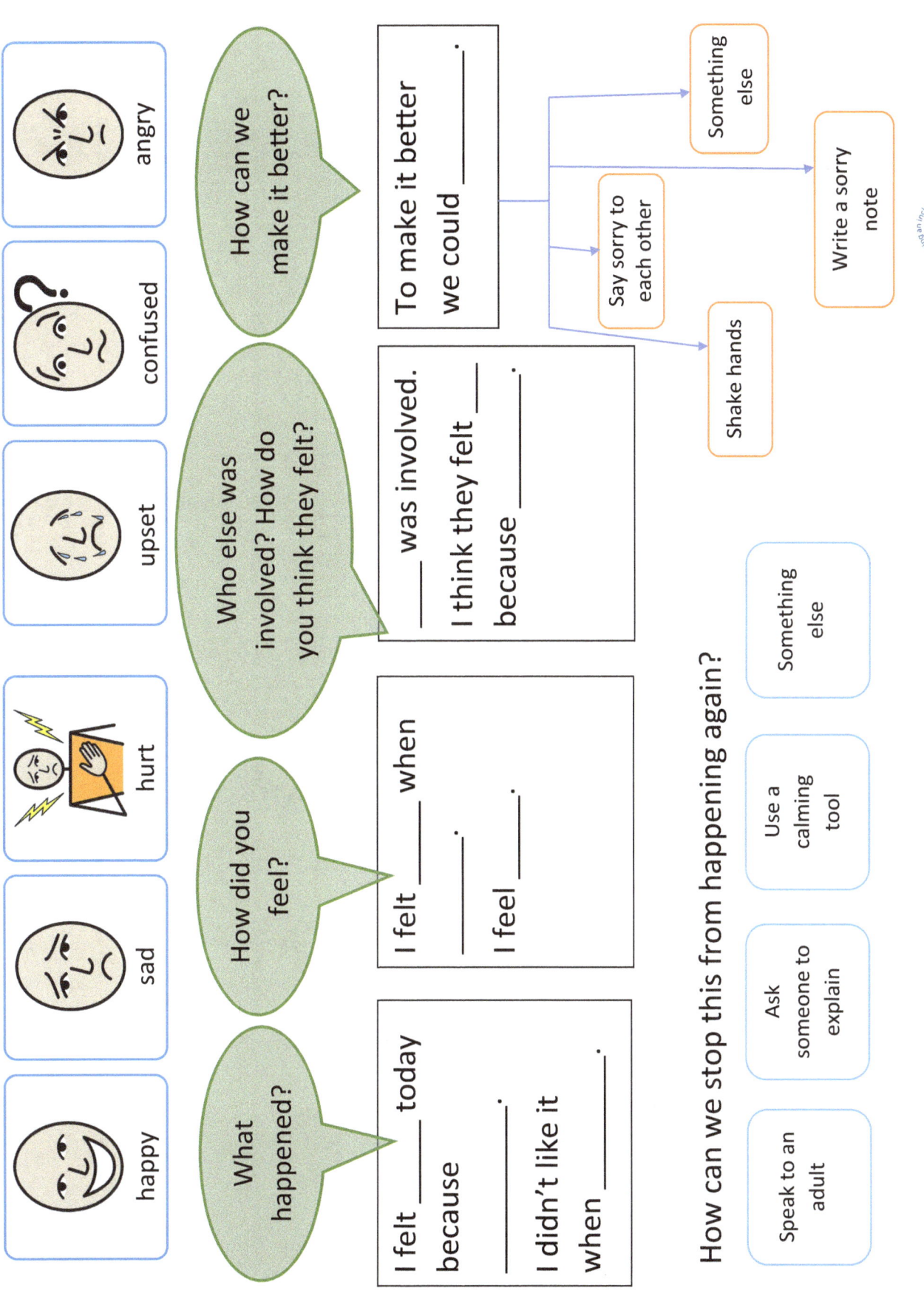

- Speak to an adult
- Ask someone to explain
- Use a calming tool
- Something else

How are you feeling?

Circle how you are feeling:

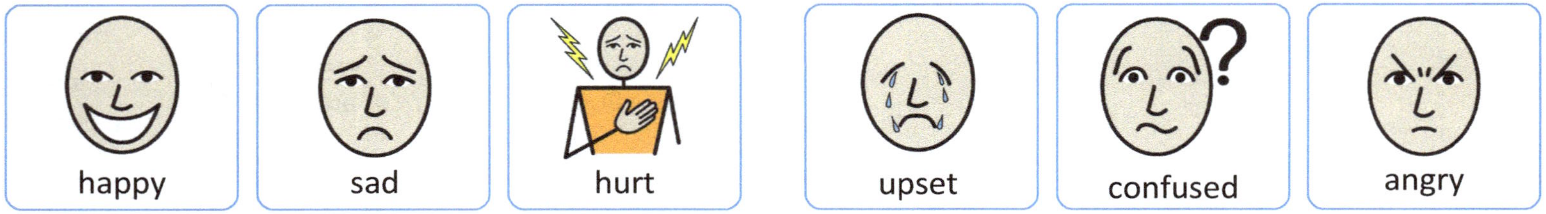

Teacher notes:

How are you feeling?

Circle how you are feeling:

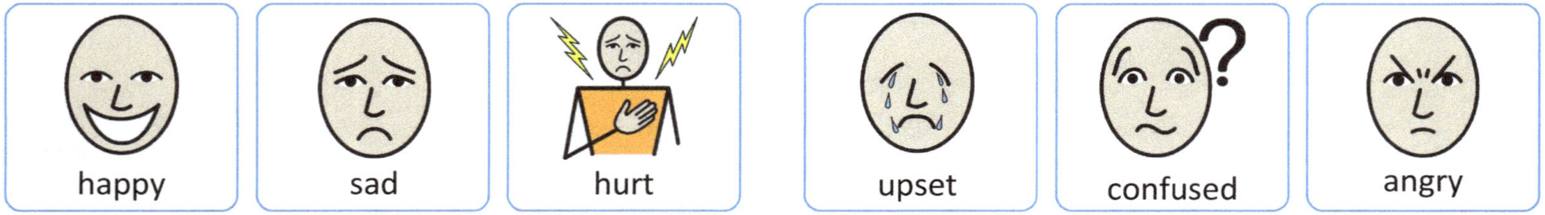

Teacher notes:

One Page Profile

Name:		Triggers:	<photo>
Stage	**What does my behaviour look like?**	**What can adults do to help?**	**What resources/strategies can I use?**
1  happy	• • • •	• • • •	• • • •
2  excited	• • • •	• • • •	• • • •
3  angry	• • • •	• • • •	• • • •
4  calm face	• • • •	• • • •	• • • •

Example One Page Profile

Name: Example	**Triggers:** • My task being too challenging • Being asked to edit my work • Being seemingly told off		<photo>
Stage	**What does my behaviour look like?**	**What can adults do to help?**	**What resources/ strategies can I use?**
1 	• I am keen to do well • I may look like I am understanding the lesson • I can sometimes daydream • With support I can achieve well in the lesson • I like to know my timetable	• Plan for regular check ins with me • Check if I have understood during the lesson • Be patient with me if I am daydreaming and just give me reminders • Consider carefully how to introduce new concepts to me and how to support me to edit my work positively.	• Visual timetable • Resources to support asking for help • Task plans
2 	• I can be fidgety and need to leave my seat • I can find it difficult to start my task • I can seem giddy and excitable • I can be very hypervigilant	• Offer a brain break or a sensory break • Ensure a visual timetable is available for me to see at all times • Give lots of praise for doing the right thing and don't get cross • Provide sentence stems/support to start my task	• Sensory circuit/ brain break • Visual timetable • Sentence stems/ scaffolds
3 	• I can leave the room • I can lash out verbally at adults and peers • I can destroy my work • I can refuse to follow any instructions. • I can sometimes cry	• Offer distractions – I love football and reading so I like talking about these or offer a reading book. • Try to find the root of the problem rather than reacting to the secondary behaviour. • Give me a safe space to go to so I can regulate. • Do not talk too much to me but offer comfort. • Don't shout at me.	• Safe space with calming activity cards • Sensory resources • A reading book or football colouring sheets
4 	• I can struggle to articulate my feelings • I can take a while to regulate myself • I can begin to tolerate adults around me • I can cry.	• Allow me time to regulate • Use visuals to support me to have a restorative conversation • Reinforce positives from the day • Comfort me if I am calm • Discuss restorative actions needed e.g. saying sorry, writing a letter, tidying the area etc	• Visual restorative conversation card/talk stems • Positive book • Zones of regulation board • Resources for restorative actions

Chapter 4

The Use of Visuals

What Does this Chapter Cover?

- The importance of visuals
- Timetables and boards
- Displays and classroom resources
- Learning tasks and activities

What Is Included in the Resources Section?

- Now and Next board
- Choice Board for families
- Needs Board for families
- Example of a Maths Task Plan (finding a fractions of a number)
- Example of a Maths Task Plan (multiplying and dividing by 10, 100 and 1000)
- Example of a Castles Vocabulary sheet
- Example of a Reading Task Plan

The Importance of Visuals

It is commonly recognised that a picture is worth a thousand words. However, when supporting students' understanding in the classroom, it is also useful to know that 'Visuals are processed **60,000 times faster** than text (Gillett, 2014, cited in Tatiana, 2022, p. 6, emphasis in original).

When explicitly teaching vocabulary or introducing new/unfamiliar words to a class, most teachers would automatically use visuals to support their explanations and the students' understanding. Children who struggle with retaining new vocabulary, including those with DLD, understand and learn better through the use of visuals rather than solely through the spoken word. As well as supporting the learning of new vocabulary, visuals can also be used effectively to support a range of other

DOI: 10.4324/9781032717869-4

concepts such as: instructions, transitions, task completion, understanding of the structure of the day, and benefit *all* children. They are permanent and therefore allow the learner to refer back to them which can reduce anxiety, can develop independence skills, allows the child time to process the information, and ensures that a child's working memory capacity is not overloaded.

For children with DLD and those who struggle with receptive language, vocabulary and working memory, visuals are vital in all areas.

Timetables and Boards

Whole-class visual timetables:

Universally, whole-class visual timetables are beneficial for several reasons. For any children in the classroom who can feel unsettled by not knowing what their day will look like, when an activity will be ending or what they will be doing next, a visual timetable can support them. It reduces anxiety as there is no uncertainty about their day and it allows children to develop independence without having to ask the teacher what is happening next.

However, simply having a visual timetable up in a classroom does not immediately reap all of these benefits and, in fact, if it is not kept up to date regularly, it can have the opposite effect as children can become *more* anxious as they are not doing what the timetable says. Taking the time to talk though the timetable and any changes to the day is extremely beneficial. This can be done in the morning for the whole day, or can be split into morning and afternoon.

To ensure that the timetable is purposeful and has the maximum impact, it is useful to have a system to show where the children are on the timetable as the day progresses. For example, the visuals could be ticked as they are finished, it could be a flap of card that closes, the card could be physically taken off and put in a 'finished' bag, it could be simply turned over or there could be an arrow that is moved down during the day. Remembering to keep up to this, although hugely important, can easily be forgotten within a teacher's busy day so it can be useful to choose a 'timetable monitor' to keep up to this at the end of each lesson. Choosing a student with DLD or autism can be useful as they are likely to be the ones who would benefit most from it being kept up to date.

Examples below:

FIGURE 4.1

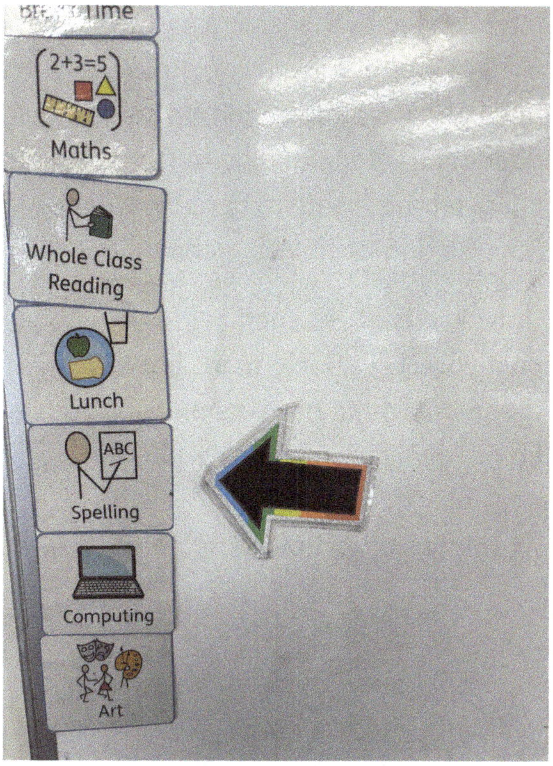

FIGURE 4.2

FIGURE 4.3

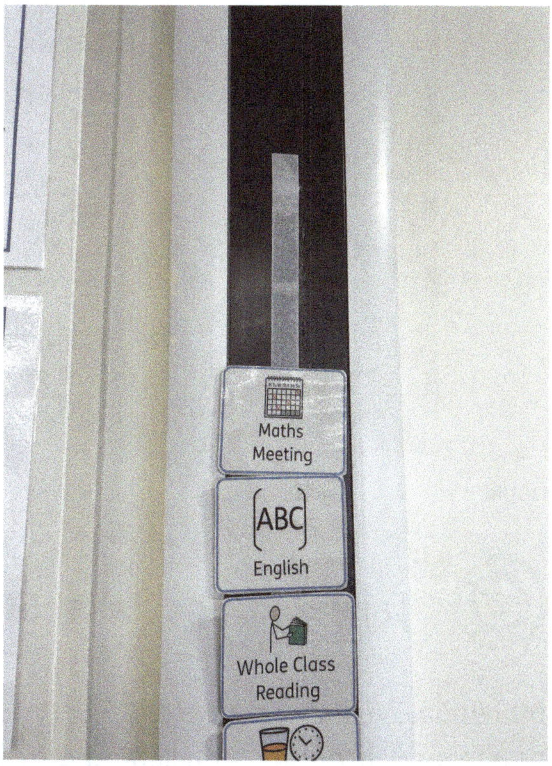

FIGURE 4.4

Whole-class needs board and choice boards:

Mainly used in the younger years in a mainstream school, needs and choice boards are vital for children who struggle with language to be able to communicate. The needs board allows them to communicate any needs they may have, for example needing the toilet, being hurt or being hungry, and so on. The choice board allows the children the freedom to make their own choices and supports them to do this if they find making decisions a challenge.

Universally, it is beneficial to have these boards up for all children to access, particularly in Early Years but also further up the school if required. However, for these boards to have a significant impact and to fully support the class, children must be explicitly taught how to use them.

Examples of a choice and needs board below:

FIGURE 4.5

Targeted/Specialist Strategies

Individual visual timetables: For some children, having the whole-class visual timetable will not be sufficient and they may require an individual one. It may also be that these children are in a separate group or access 1:1 interventions and, therefore, the whole-class timetable may not reflect everything that will be in their day. A child who has difficulty with language may find the concept of time difficult, therefore using an individual visual timetable could reduce any anxiety, enabling the child to focus on the task, help them to learn the language of time and cope with routines more independently (Elks and McLachlan, 2009, p. 16).

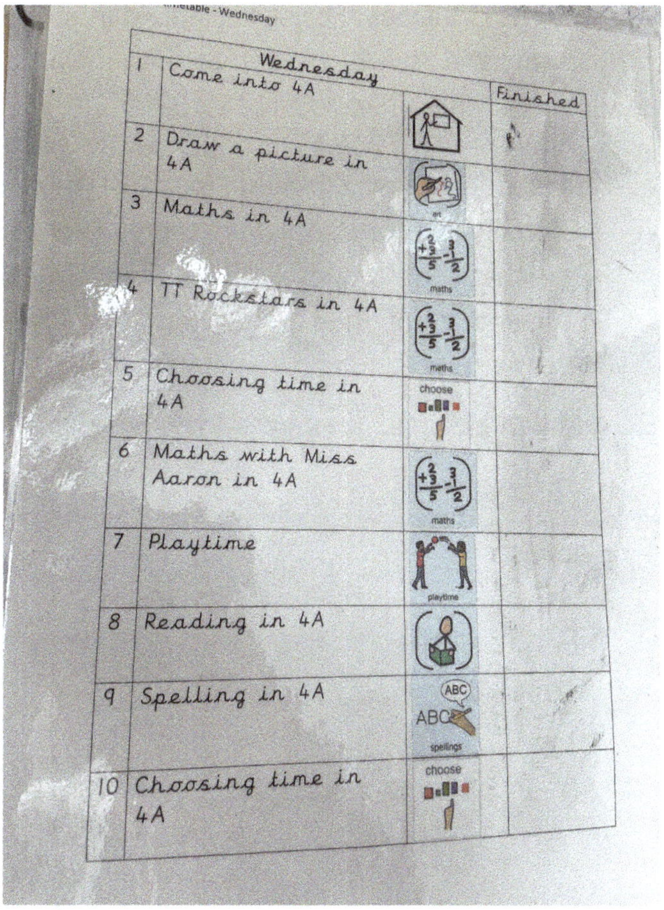

FIGURE 4.6

These children may benefit from having an individual visual timetable with the following considerations:

- Would a whole day or weekly timetable be overwhelming, and would they benefit from having a separate one for the morning and one for the afternoon?
- Although having the visual of the activity on the timetable is important, some children may also benefit from having the picture of the adult who they will be with alongside it.
- Consider the system in which the child will show that the session has finished. For example, will they tick it once it is completed? Will they take it off the timetable and put it in a bag labelled 'finished'? For children with more complex needs, they may benefit from actually taking the card with them to the session (e.g. a phonic group) and then bring it back with them and put in a finished bag.

FIGURE 4.7

Now and next boards: For some individuals, their needs may be so that they require a simple now and next board rather than the whole day on the timetable. These can be used in a number of ways for:

- A lesson (e.g. **now**: complete task one, **next**: complete task two)
- An activity (e.g. **now**: draw the table, **next**: fill in the information)
- For motivation (e.g. **now**: maths, **next**: choosing time)
- Focus and attention (e.g. **now**: 5 minutes of science, **next**: 3-minute break)

Below is an example of a now and next board:

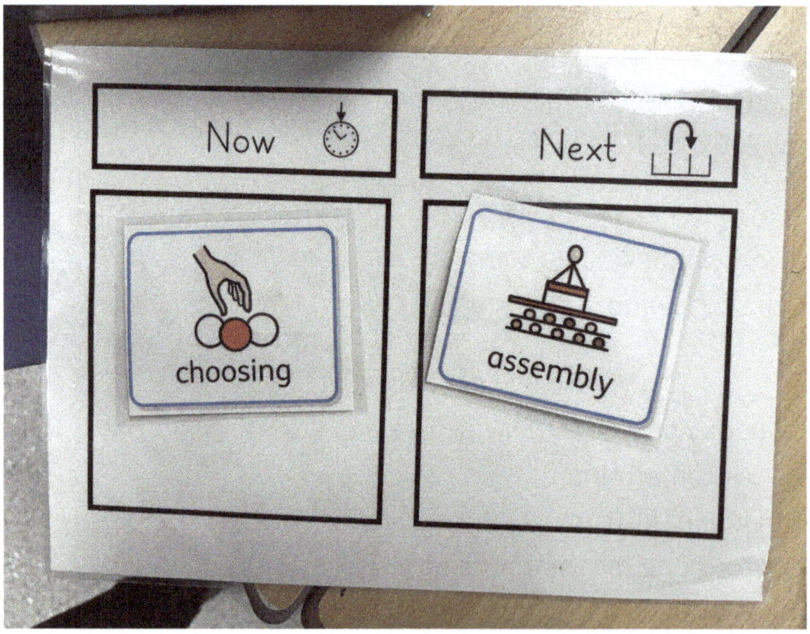

FIGURE 4.8

Individual needs and choice boards: For many children, having a whole-class needs/choice board may be enough and they may be able to access this independently. However, there are likely to be children who require a more targeted/specialist approach. For these children, having individual needs or choice boards can support them to develop their independence and it allows the boards to be bespoke to them, for example the needs that they have or the choices being activities that the teacher knows that they enjoy.

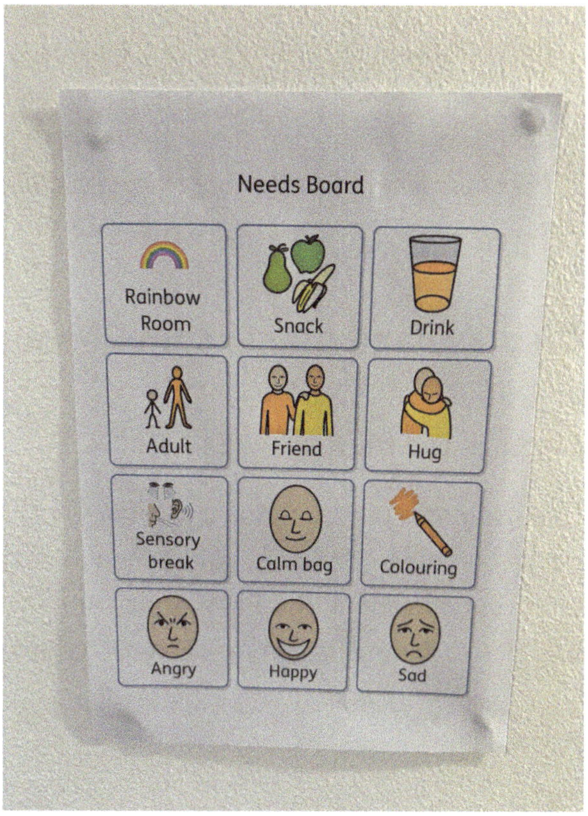

FIGURE 4.9

Using a choice board can enable a child to communicate their choices without the pressure of using language. However, the adult should model the appropriate language so that in time, they can begin to verbalise their choices independently (Elks and McLachlan, 2009, p. 15).

Parents, Carers and Families

For some children, the uncertainty of unstructured times at home or the inability to be able to communicate their needs or wants effectively can sometimes present itself as unwanted behaviours at home. To support families with this, schools could consider sending the following home:

- Visual timetables for routines (e.g. morning/ bedtime routine).
- Now and next visuals for tricky times (e.g. dinner times – *Now: eat at the table, next: play a game* or when the adult is making tea and the child wants attention – *Now: watching TV, Next: Dad will come and sit with you*).
- Choice boards for unstructured times when children are finding it a challenge to focus and want the adult's attention.
- Needs board for families of children with more complex needs who are unable to communicate.

For these strategies to have the most impact at home, it is important that families are taught about the importance of visuals, what the benefits are and how to use them effectively. This can be done through information sheets and/or workshops provided in school.

Examples of a now and next board and both a choice board and a needs board for families can be found in the resources section at the end of this chapter.

Reflection: *Think about the educational setting that you work in. Do you use visual timetables and boards? Are they being used effectively and purposefully or more as a display? Consider how you can work together with staff and families to ensure maximum impact and support for the children.*

Displays and Classroom Resources

Displays and working walls:

Ensuring that all vocabulary displayed is accompanied by visuals, supports understanding and enables children to revisit and access the new vocabulary. This is more common in the Early Years and into Key Stage 1 but can tend to disappear in Key Stage 2, despite being the years when vocabulary becomes much more complex.

Resources:

Labelling resources with the word and the visual around the classroom is beneficial for those students who find language and/or reading a challenge and encourages independence. Again, this is seen commonly in the Early Years, but it can peter out as the student moves through school.

FIGURE 4.10

Routines:

Having visuals to support routines can develop independence and reduce working memory capacity. These can be for any routines in the classroom, for example: putting your wellies on (picture below), hanging your coat up in a morning, washing your hands or how to write the date in your book.

FIGURE 4.11

Learning Tasks and Activities

'Good teaching for pupils with SEND is good teaching for all' (Davies and Henderson, 2020, p. 9). The EEF state that strong evidence was found to suggest that high quality teaching for pupils with SEND is firmly based on strategies that will 'either already be in the repertoire of every mainstream teacher or can be relatively easily added to it' (Davies and Henderson, 2020, p. 20).

The strategies that are highlighted below to support children to access learning tasks and activities by supporting vocabulary and using visuals are unlikely to be new to any teacher but can easily get forgotten about or overlooked due to teacher workload. However, these strategies can be hugely beneficial for those with DLD and for all.

Whole-class task plans:

Providing a visual task plan for every lesson can seem an overwhelming idea but there are ways that this can be done that does not have to impact workload. The purpose of a task plan is to have a visual representation of the task that children can refer to, so they know what the task involves and it also develops independence. This does not mean that it has to be typed up, colourful or laminated, and so on. See, below, two ways that this can be done:

- **Written on the board:** Task plans can be created as part of the teaching process. They can be done with the class when you are modelling how to complete an activity, for example, finding a fraction of a number (see photo). The teacher can then model how to use the task plan when working out example calculations as part of the lesson input.

  These can be left up on the board for the lesson. A photo can also be taken to do either of the following:
  - Put up on a maths display to keep for the class to refer to when recapping
  - Stick in the back of children's maths books to refer to when/if needed in the future

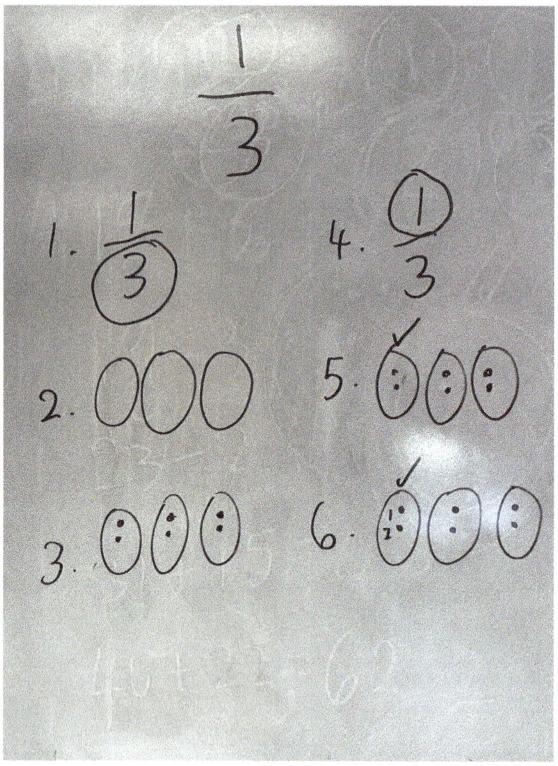

FIGURE 4.12

- **Added to lesson PowerPoints:** An extra slide can be added to the lesson PowerPoint which can be used as part of the input and then displayed during the independent task. Again, these can be printed off to keep for children to refer to. They could be put on display or made into cards or a book of task plans for specific topics, for example 'Fractions', 'conjunctions' or 'answering inferential questions.'

Images and visuals for whole-class learning:

All children learn in different ways and have strengths in different areas. To ensure that all children in a class are catered for and can access the learning, it is beneficial to use images and visuals alongside any audio information. As mentioned at the beginning of the chapter, 'Visuals are processed 60,000 times faster than text' (Gillett, 2014, cited in Tatiana, 2022, p. 6) and so using visuals is a vital component to the learning process. Most teachers are fully aware of this and how these can be used in the classroom. It is just about making sure that this is at the forefront when teaching, particularly when introducing something new. For example, using diagrams to explain maths concepts or to support visualisation of word problems, using images/photographs when introducing new vocabulary and using visuals to support creative writing ideas.

Word banks and vocabulary mats:

These are well-known in schools. However, it can be something that (a) can easily be forgotten about and (b) can be used ineffectively. Again, providing word banks and vocabulary mats for every lesson can feel unmanageable and teachers can fall into the trap of printing off 'topic' word banks and vocabulary mats which may not have the exact vocabulary needed and do not always have visuals on, so children still require an adult to read the words to them or explain what they are. However, if we consider that the purpose of word banks and vocabulary mats are to support vocabulary development and to develop children's independence, this method is not an ideal one. See below for some strategies that can have maximum impact for the child but minimum impact on workload.

- **Classroom displays:** Vocabulary can be explored as a class and displays can be developed overtime, for example topic words (Tier 3) can be explored during the lessons and added to the display with visuals and prompts around the word. The classroom could also have a Tier 2 display/word wall in which words are regularly explored in the classroom either as part of a lesson or a specific vocabulary lesson. These words can again be added to the word wall along with a visual and other information (e.g. synonyms/antonyms etc.).
- **Lesson activity:** As part of the lesson, one of the activities could include creating a word bank for the independent task. This could involve having a blank PowerPoint slide and discussing what vocabulary may be needed for the task. Pictures could be drawn next to the word as they are written, or pictures could be added if there is time. This slide can then be up on the board during the task. This

could also be done by drawing on the board. This word bank could then be printed off (or a photo taken of the vocabulary on the board) and kept for future lessons: displayed on the wall or made into a large class dictionary.

- **Vocabulary station:** Rather than producing a word bank for each lesson, the classroom could have a 'Vocabulary station' where words are written on card with a visual alongside and categorised into groups to support children to find the right words. For example, an information text vocabulary sheet, vocabulary linked to 'Castles' or maths operations and so on. These sheets could include both Tier 3 and Tier 2 vocabulary.

Sentence stems:

Many children can find the idea of a blank page a daunting thought. Providing sentence stems for children that they can 'choose to use' can support confidence, independence and can support those children who may find it a challenge to start a sentence. They can also support children to include higher level vocabulary in their work and model to them how these words are used in a sentence. Providing these does not have to impact on workload as again, these can either be created during the teacher input (although it can be beneficial to pre-think them if you are wanting the higher level vocabulary to be used effectively as it can be a challenge to think these sentences up on the spot!), added to the PowerPoint and left on the board or added to an independent sheet to refer to.

Targeted/Specialist Strategies

There will inevitably be some children in the class, including those with DLD, who will require extra, targeted support to access the learning tasks. See below for some examples of how these children can be supported:

Individual word banks/ vocabulary sheets: It can be beneficial to have a way of recording vocabulary that these children need individually. This can be done in several ways, including:

- Starting with a blank sheet of paper stuck on the table in their place where words that they find difficult can be recorded and the teacher (or the child) can add a drawing or a picture can be printed to stick next to it. As words come up that the child struggles with, words can continue to be added.

- Having a vocabulary card in which children can again add any words on that they are struggling with, including a small picture. This card can be kept in their drawer or with their belongings and taken with them to different lessons, and so on, and used when needed.
- A vocabulary book (or personal dictionary) can be used again to record words that the child is finding challenging individually. Words can be added and the child can add pictures and extra information if appropriate, for example synonyms/ antonyms and so on.

If children do require an individual word bank or vocabulary mat, it is useful if the words have visuals alongside them and that the words are categorised to support the child to be able to use the resource independently. For example, for a character description, they can be sorted into words for the eyes, hair, body, personality, and so on, and include a visual.

Individual prompts: There may be concepts that individual children require support with, for example writing 'b' and 'd' the correct way. It can be useful to have these on their tables or on card to keep with their belongings. Any individual prompts that are provided need explicitly teaching as a method to the child/ren if they are to be used effectively and have the greatest impact.

Individual/ group task plans: There may be times when individuals or groups of children may need a task plan either for a differentiated task or to further explain an aspect of a lesson that they struggle with. For example, in a reading lesson, when children are answering questions, it may be beneficial for some children to have a task plan to work through:

1. Read the text
2. Read the question
3. Find the answer in the text
4. Underline it
5. Write it

Again, these individual or group task plans have the most impact when (a) they are accompanied by visuals so children can use them independently without having to ask an adult what it says or means and (b) these children are explicitly taught how to use them.

Reflection: *Think about how often word banks, vocabulary mats and task plans are provided for the children in your setting. Is the vocabulary accompanied by visuals and are they being used effectively?*

Parents, Carers and Families

Between 50–70% of children with DLD will have at least one family member with DLD (NIH, National Institute on Deafness and other communication disorders). This is worth considering when providing homework tasks as often, if the child struggles, they will ask their families for support who may themselves struggle with language. See below for some ways in which families can be supported to help their child with their homework:

Homework sheets can be amended to include:

- **Word banks/vocabulary mats:** These could be included as part of the homework sheet. Teachers could have a blank template which is simply populated with the necessary vocabulary for that week's homework task. These should include visuals alongside the words.
- **Task plans:** Many adults at home, particularly in maths, are concerned that they are teaching their child methods that they were taught at school instead of how they do it in the classroom so task plans are really useful for this. It is also beneficial to include an example.

Homework can be a very stressful task for many families, particularly if a child has a language difficulty. For children with DLD, it may be useful to consider whether it is appropriate to send the same homework as the rest of class and what the purpose of the homework is for the individual.

Homework that is heavily reliant on families supporting them (a) can be too hard and overwhelming for them, (b) will not teach the child anything and (c) can significantly affect self-esteem and confidence and have an adverse effect on the child's attitude to learning. It is better to give them a simple homework task that they can access, rather than a more complex task that they do not complete at all (Speech and Language UK, 2023, p. 28). See below for ideas for alternative homework tasks for children with DLD:

- Opportunities for 'talking homework' with their family may be more valuable for children with DLD than a written comprehension task (Speech and Language UK, 2023, p. 28). Children could be provided with 'talk tasks' for homework about anything covered in school to help them practice formulating sentences. These tasks could include things such as:
  - Describing a picture to a member of their family using focus adjectives.
  - Creating and then describing a maths pattern to a family member.
  - Telling their family what they have learnt so far about a Romans topic using focus vocabulary.
  - Going on walks and discussing what they see using focus conjunctions.
  - Playing their favourite game at home and discussing three reasons why it is their favourite.

  The possibilities are endless and depends on the current topics in school and the individual child.
- For written homework, it can be helpful to base the tasks on the child's interests. This can help to motivate them to complete them at home. For example:
  - Designing their ideal bedroom and labelling it with what would be in it, adding adjectives.
  - Creating a maths game and writing instructions for it.
  - Creating an imaginary animal made up from three other animals and writing a fact file for them (e.g. what do they eat? where do they live? what do they look like? etc.).
  - Inventing a new machine (e.g. a machine that can make your tea, make your bed, go to the shops for you etc.) and writing an explanation as to how it works.
  - Putting together a treasure hunt for a member of their family to follow. This could be in the house or in the garden and children could write clues to find certain objects.
- Children with DLD work incredibly hard in school and will find just being in lessons all day overwhelming enough. They would benefit from not having lots of homework tasks. It could be beneficial for them to focus solely on aspects that they will need throughout their school life (e.g. spellings and timestables). See below for fun activities that families could do to teach these:

  Timestables:
  - Calculations could be stuck on the wall going down the stairs so the children say the answer every time they walk up or down the stairs.
  - Board games could be created together with their families where they land on a coloured square and pick a question.

- Timestables games could be played including bingo games, games based on noughts and crosses and partner games.
- Snap dragons can be made with calculations added on that they can play with family members or friends at home.

Spellings:

- Children could write/ draw the spellings in funny writing/bubble writing.
- Making mnemonics for the spellings can be a fun way of remembering how to spell a word (e.g. **b**ig **e**lephants **c**an **a**lways **u**nderstand **s**mall **e**lephants (because) or **p**eople **e**at **o**range **p**eel **l**ike **e**lephants (people)). Children can have fun making up funny alternatives.
- A family member can put the words up on the wall/around the room/garden and say the words and the child must run and touch that word. This can also be reversed so the child reads the word and the family member runs.
- The words could be created by cutting letters out from a magazine or a newspaper and sticking them on a new piece of paper.

Any of the above activities that are sent home must be discussed with families, so they are aware of the purpose and the expectation of the homework task. It may also be necessary to send home a task plan for the adult, so they fully understand the activity. This will ensure maximum impact for the child.

Examples of task plans and a vocabulary sheet on can be found in the resources section at the end of this chapter.

Reflection: *Consider the types of homework tasks that are sent home for children with DLD or how many families express concerns about their child struggling with homework.*

Consider the purpose of the homework and if there a better task that they can access which can have a greater impact on their learning and also increase self-esteem and confidence.

Key Takeaways from Chapter 4

- **Visuals are processed 60,000 times faster** than text and are beneficial in all aspects of school and home life e.g. displays, timetables, vocabulary development and for routines.
- It is **vital to use visuals** in the classroom both universally and on a targeted level as they can support children to communicate their needs and wants, can support them with their learning and their understanding of vocabulary and can reduce anxiety.
- **Good teaching for pupils with SEND is good teaching for all!**
- Many children with DLD can have **at least one family member with DLD**. This is worth considering when communicating with families and when planning homework tasks.

References

EEF (2020). Special Educational Needs in Mainstream Schools. Guidance Report. Education Endowment Foundation. Available at: https://educationendowmwntfoundation.org.uk/education-evidence/guidance-reports/send [accessed 7 April 2024].

Elks, L. and McLachlan, H. (2009). *Early Language Builders: Advice and Activities to Encourage Pre-school Children's Communication Skills*. ELKLAN.

National Institute on Deafness and Other Communication Disorders (n.d.). What Causes DLD? Available at https://www.nidcd.nih.gov/health/developmental-language-disorder#:~:text=Neurodevelopmental%20disorders%20tend%20to%20run,family%20member%20with%20the%20disorder [accessed 7 April 2024].

Speech and Language UK (2023). *Developmental Language Disorder. A Guide for Every Teacher on Supporting Children and Young People with Developmental Language Disorder (DLD) in Mainstream Schools*. Available at https://speechandlanguage.org.uk/wp-content/uploads/2023/12/ican_dld_guide_final_aug4.pdf [accessed 7 April 2024].

Tatiana, F. (2022). *Visual Communication and Digital Media: Exploring the Science behind Visual Communication in Digital Age*. Master's thesis.

Chapter 4

Resources Section

Task Plan – Multiplying and Dividing by 10, 100 and 1000

H	T	O •	10th	100th	1000th
		•			
		•			

x 10			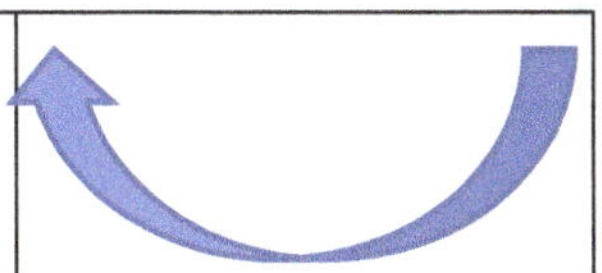
x 100			
x 1000		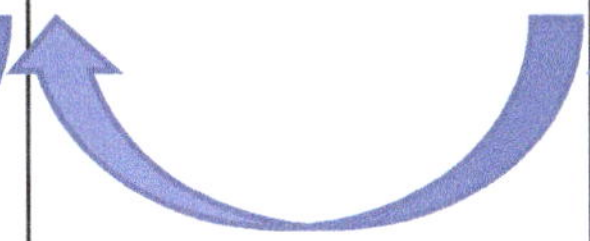	
÷ 10			
÷ 100			
÷ 1000			

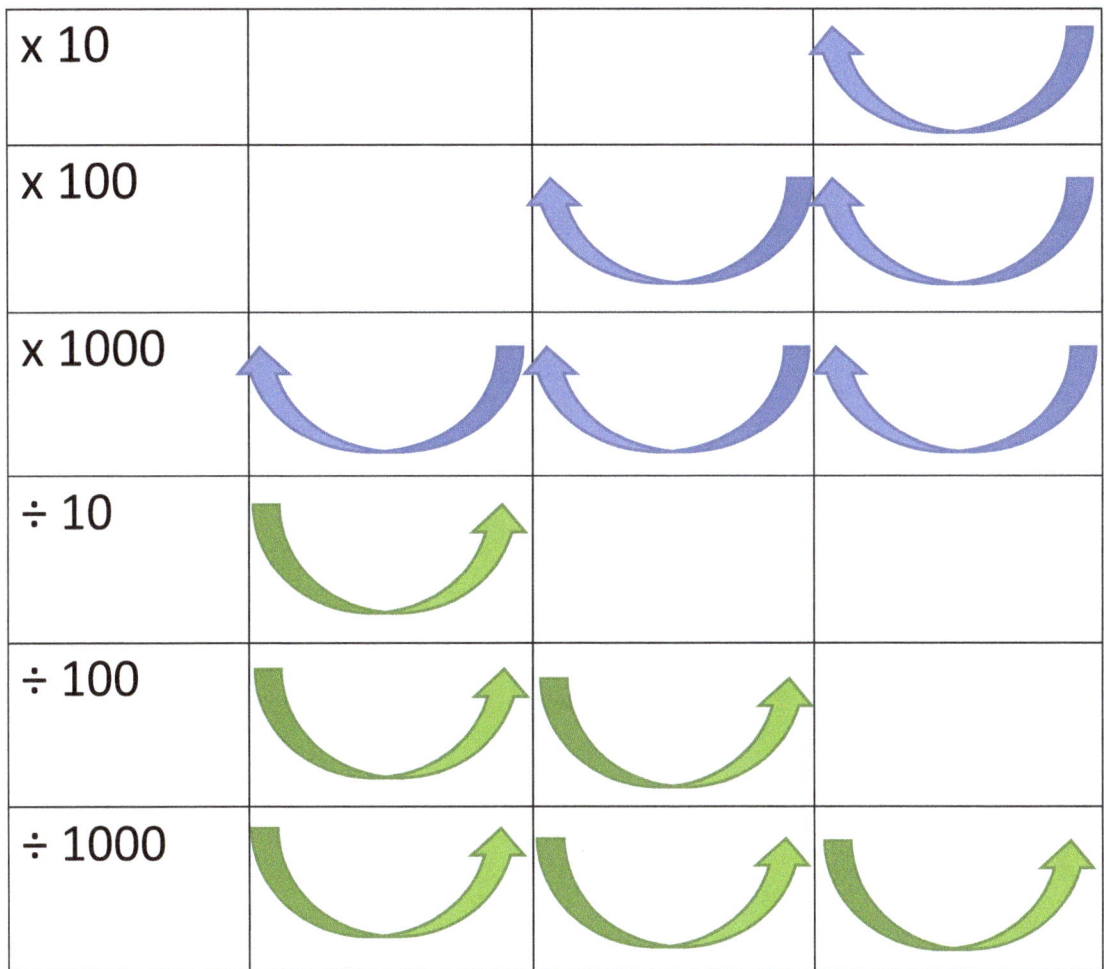

Remember!
The decimal point never moves

Now 

Next 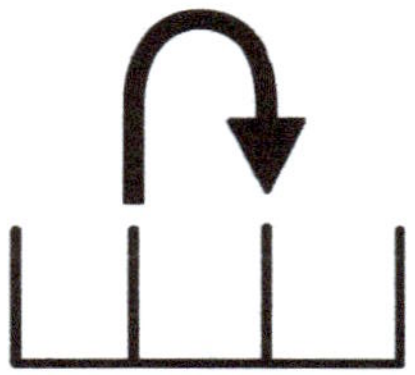

Family Choice Board

This choice board can be used for when your child needs to entertain themselves at home independently. As the adult, you can choose which of these options you give. These cards can either be cut out or the ones you do not require can be covered up.

Read a book

Play a game

Listen to music

iPad time

Play in the garden

Play with toys

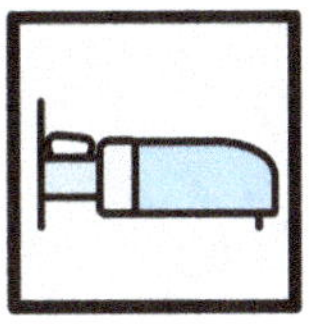

Play in bedroom

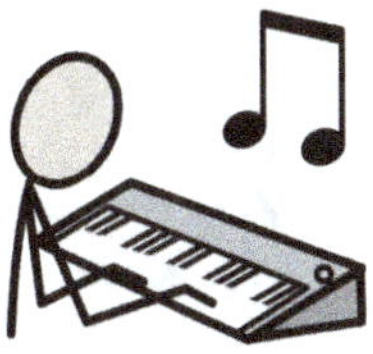

Play a musical instrument

Drawing

Painting

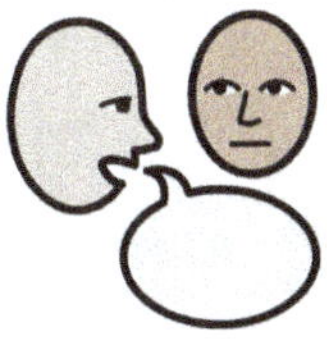

Talk to brother or sister

Watch TV

Family Needs Board

A needs board can be beneficial for any child who is yet to be able to communicate verbally or who is struggling to communicate their needs effectively.

The cards below can be introduced to your child starting with the top line, so they are able to communicate their basic needs.

Slowly the rest can be introduced to support communication at home.

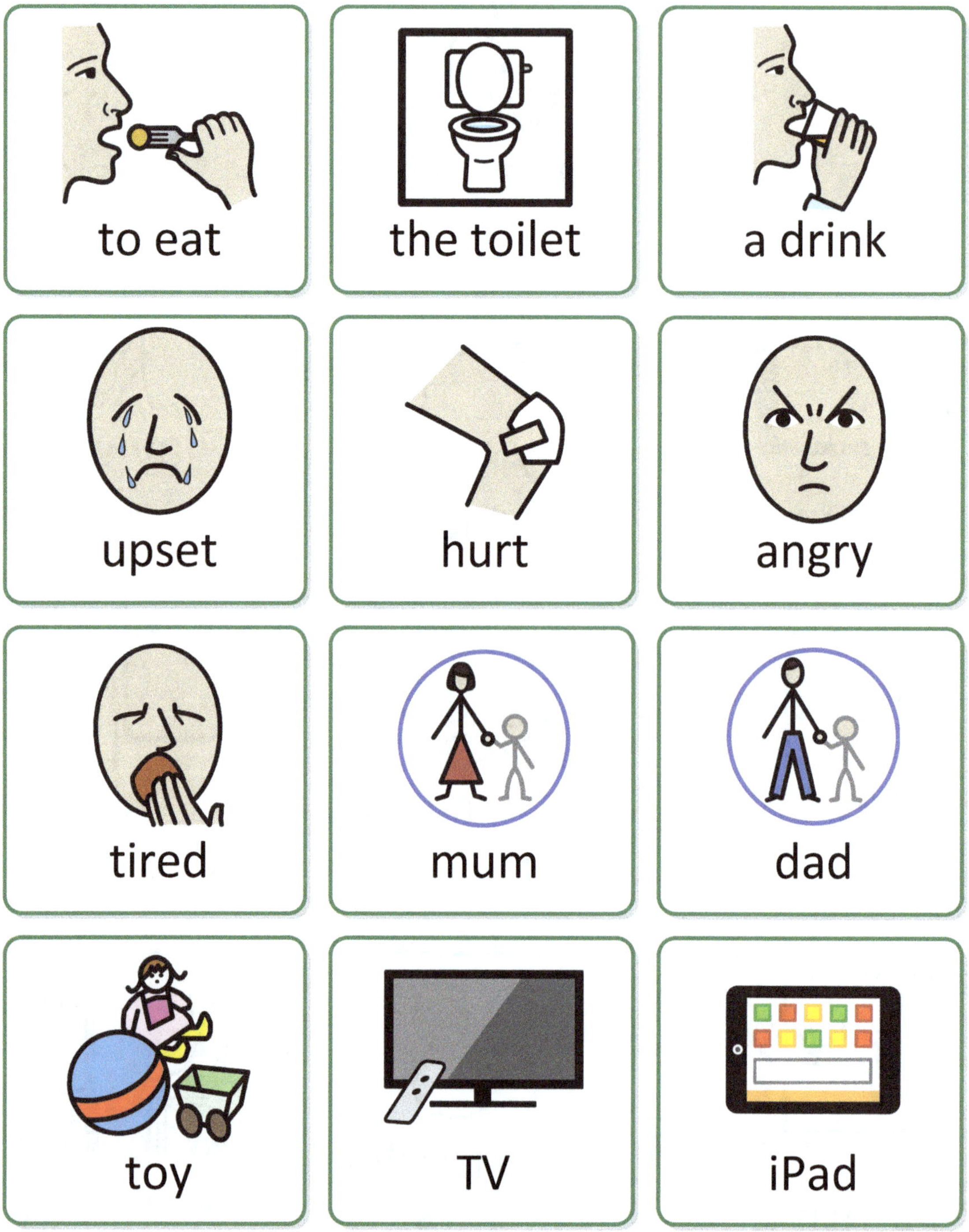

Maths Lesson Task Plan – finding fractions

Circle the denominator	$\frac{7}{10 \leftarrow}$
Divide the whole by that number	÷
Circle the numerator	$\frac{7 \leftarrow}{10}$
Multiply by that number	×
Write your answer	

Castles Vocabulary

banquet	
ancient	
furniture	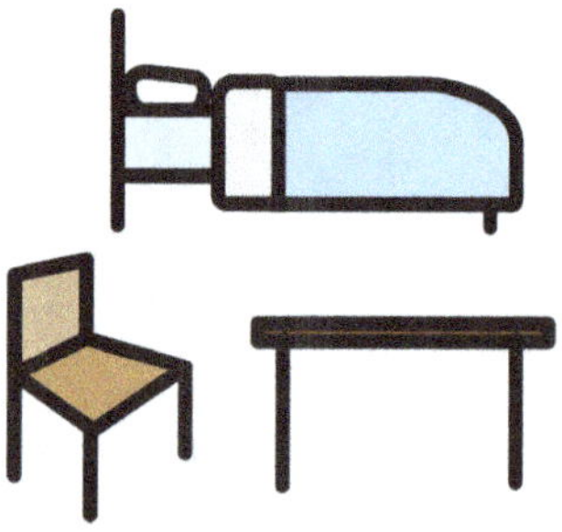
grounds	
corridors	

Reading Lesson Task Plan

Read the text	
Read the question	
Find the answer in text	
Underline it	
Write it	

Chapter 5

Transition

What Does this Chapter Cover?

- Ensuring a sense of safety and security
- Developing positive relationships and a sense of belonging
- Strategies to support the primary to secondary school transition process

What Is Included in the Resources Section?

- 'Transition' social story
- Blank 'Meet the Teacher' sheet
- Talk stems to support asking for help at secondary school

Transition

Transitions can be an anxious time for all children and young people, whether they are transitioning to a new classroom and class teacher within the primary school or to another school setting. To best support all children, this process should be carefully planned and thoroughly thought through to ensure it is a smooth and positive process.

For children with Developmental Language Disorder, transitions can cause a significant amount of anxiety, particularly when transitioning from primary to secondary school and extra effort should be made to avoid adverse social, emotional and educational outcomes (White, 2020). Despite some children with DLD appearing to meet expectations in primary school with the additional support that they have received, underlying language difficulties can resurface with the huge increase in the demands of secondary school (Leaver, 2023). However, with a highly bespoke transition with additional visits and scaffolds for new routines, all children with SEND can thrive (Mould, 2021).

The Education Endowment Foundation (EEF) describe a 'trio of challenges' regarding transition, one of which is linked to school routines and expectations. They state

DOI: 10.4324/9781032717869-5

that successful transitions have close cross-phase links and include a variety of opportunities for taster days and visits so children can become familiar with the building, the routines and incorporate time for extra explanations, practice and reinforcement of routines (Mould, 2021).

If we consider Maslow's hierarchy of needs which comprises of a five-tier model of human needs and is often depicted as levels within a pyramid (Maslow, 1943, 1954, cited in McLeod, 2007), once a child has all physiological needs met (such as oxygen, food and water), the subsequent needs which come into play are for safety and security and for a sense of belonging and relationships. When planning for transition, these needs should be considered, and the following questions asked:

Safety and security	Relationships and a sense of belonging
• What will stay the same? • What will be different? • When will the changes happen? • What does the building look like and where everything is (including the toilets)? • How many visits they will have and what will happen on these visits? • When they will start and what will happen on the first day? • Who is their teacher, and will there be any other key adults that they will work with? • What will the rules for behaviour be including where they can and can't go and what they can and can't do? • Which of their friends will they be with on transition day?	• What can we do in advance to make the child feel as comfortable as possible to come to our school/class? • How can we begin to develop a nurturing relationship based on trust? • How can we show that we are on the child's 'team' and want the best for them? • How can we create a 'safe and inclusive' environment? • What can we put in place for the child to be able to communicate anything that they are struggling with? • How can we make sure that good communication is prioritised? • What seemingly small things can be done to ensure the best possible outcomes?

The following are some answers to these questions and ideas for supporting a successful transition process on a universal level:

A Whole-class Transition Social Story

Social stories are a great way of communicating simply to the whole class about transition. They can be used to explore different feelings that may arise during the transition period and reassure the children that it is okay (and normal) to feel this way. During a period where there is a lot of anxiety around change, it is also a good opportunity to highlight to the children all the things that will be staying the same.

Although there will be more aspects staying the same when transitioning within the primary school, there are still likely to be *some* things staying the same even when transitioning to a secondary provision, for example, their morning routine, friends who are going to the same school and the lessons they will have.

Reading this story daily for a week or two before transition day, ensuring that it is 'frequent enough to be effective and infrequent enough to avoid needless repetition' (Gray, 2015, p. lxiii), can make sure that children have all the necessary information and feel ready and supported.

Primary to Secondary School:

If it is possible to get information from the secondary school about transition day, including which adults they will meet (e.g. the Year 7 team), what they will do on transition day and what the building look like (including some pictures of areas such as the main doorway and where they will eat etc.), a social story could be created and would be beneficial for the Year 6 children transitioning to secondary school.

Meet the Teacher Sheets

To further support the development of positive relationships with new adults, school can send home 'Meet the Teacher' sheets about the new class teacher and any other staff that may regularly work with the children, for example a teaching assistant. These sheets can include a photograph of the teacher/teaching assistant and then have information about them, for example their favourite colour, pets, and their favourite place to go on holiday. The purpose of these is for the child to have something to refer to over the holidays to reassure them and begin to connect with their new adults by finding things that they have in common. Including a sentence about how much you are looking forward to teaching the children and their new class in September can begin to create that feeling of belonging.

Primary to Secondary School:

For children in Year 6 transitioning to secondary school, if it is possible to gain this information from the Year 7 team, creating 'Meet the teacher' sheets for the Year 6 children would be hugely beneficial so they feel like they are already building a relationship and getting to know a member of staff in their new school.

Building Relationships

Developing nurturing relationships and communicating to all children that staff value those relationships is invaluable. In the run-up to transition day/week, this can be done in several ways. New teachers can begin to make a point of 'popping' into the class, giving any children they see a thumbs up or a big smile. Making a point of acknowledging any of the children in your new class develops that sense of belonging, develops the relationship, and communicates to the child that you are a 'safe' person who will create that 'safe and inclusive' environment for them in class next year.

In collaboration with the previous teacher, it could be arranged for new teachers to come and teach short sessions in their current classroom, for example reading a story to them or doing a 'fun' activity in their familiar environment where the only change is the new teacher.

Learning all the names of the children in your new class can be challenging at first but can have a significant impact on the relationship you have with them. When you smile, give them a thumbs up, come into their classroom and you refer to them by their name, it communicates to them that you care about them.

Primary to Secondary School:

Arranging as many visits as possible for Year 6 students to visit their new schools but also for members of the Year 7 team to visit and spend time with the children in their primary school supports the development of relationships. This ensures that they have a 'key adult' in their new school who they can talk to if needed and encourages a positive and relatively stress-free transition to a secondary provision.

The EEF also highlight the importance of healthy peer networks when supporting a positive transition amongst children (Mould, 2021). Where possible, arranging events, activities or clubs that involve Year 6 students from around the local area, including feeder schools to the local secondary schools, can promote the development of relationships with other children of the same age in the area who may go to the same secondary school as them. This can help relieve children's anxiety around leaving their friends who they have been at primary school with for so long.

Sharing the Transition Plan

The majority of a child's anxiety around transition can stem from the unknown. Children will have questions such as 'Where will they go in the morning?', 'Where will they hang their coat?', 'Where will they be sitting, and will it be near their friends?'.

Often, many of these things are *ironed out* on the transition day and then for those who need it, this information is used in transition booklets. However, because it is vital that the transition day in the summer term is successful and that no children have a negative experience of it to make the transition a positive one, putting the time in prior to the transition day can make things run smoother in the long run.

There a variety of ways this information could be shared with the class prior to transition day:

- The new teacher could visit the class prior to transition day and talk through what will happen and answer any questions.
- The new teacher could pass all the information onto the previous teacher to share with the class and take any questions.
- The new teacher could create a simple booklet with all the information on to send home with the class.

Additionally, letting the children know that they will do something fun or exciting first thing in the morning on transition day (for example an art activity or a science experiment) can ensure that the children are excited and looking forward to going to their new class.

Primary to Secondary School:

For those children moving to secondary school, it would be useful to find out the plan for the day for them and to find out as much information as possible to share with them prior to transition day. If the information is readily available, it would also be beneficial for the children to know whether they will be with their friends during the day.

Transition Day

If the work has gone into the preparations for transition (including the strategies listed above), when it comes to transition day, most children will be not only prepared and ready, but excited to see the new teacher.

Keep in mind that the focus on transition day, however tempting as a teacher, is not to test the children but to develop relationships, instil a sense of belonging and ensure that all children feel safe and secure in your classroom. The behaviour policy should be followed while also continuing to build positive relationships. Teachers can fall into the trap of wanting to be more lenient on transition day, but *all* children need boundaries to feel safe so every effort should be made to stick closely to the policy. Even with robust behaviour policies in place, there can be some differences from teacher to teacher so ensuring that the 'rules' have been clearly explained (with simple visuals as a reminder where possible) and can be referred to during the day is useful.

Transition Meetings

Typically, transition meetings are used to discuss levels and children's needs and so on, but thought should also be put into ensuring that the new teacher knows everything about every child.

Universally, things to consider are:

- Children who do not have additional needs but who have had extra support, e.g. <Name> *is fine in lessons but likes you to have a quick check in at the beginning of the independent task.*
- Any provision put in place that the class have responded positively to, e.g. routines at different times of the day (e.g. morning, after break times), the way instructions are given, certain visuals that have been used to support volume in the classroom etc.

In September

If the educational setting you work in has an electronic system to communicate with families, it may also be nice to send a message to all children in your new class prior to them starting in September, telling them how excited you are for the new school year and maybe a picture of the classroom all set up ready or of something exciting that you will be doing. The suspense and excitement could be further created by sending a picture of something hidden that they will find out about when they come into school, for example a letter or a parcel addressed to them.

Targeted/ Specialist strategies

There are some skills that children with DLD can struggle with that are important during transition, for example, receptive language and processing instructions, formulating sentences, asking questions and understanding higher level vocabulary. A study in 2022 found that transition support for children with DLD should focus predominantly on emotion recognition skill (Kenyon, Palikara and Lucas, 2022).

Below are some strategies that can be used during times of transition on a more targeted/specialised level:

Group or individual activities: New teachers and/or teaching assistants can plan short activities with any children on the Special Educational Needs (SEN) register or for any children who they feel would benefit from extra transition. This could be simply reading them a story at the end of the day or completing activities that they enjoy, for example art activities. The purpose of these groups would be to further develop a relationship with these children, letting them know that you are a safe person and care about them and to put them at ease for the transition. It is also an opportunity to get to know these children better – what they enjoy and also what they don't.

The two-minute relationship builder: In a 2013 ASCD educational leadership conference, presenter Grace Dearborn shared the 'Two-by-Ten' strategy which promotes establishing an initial connection and forming the foundations for a sustainable relationship (McKibben, 2014). This strategy involves spending two minutes a day for ten days with a child and can be used for any children who it is felt would benefit from this, for example any children with DLD but also children with autism, ADHD and/or challenging behaviours.

Transition booklets: All schools are familiar with transition booklets and they are a vital part of transition for all children who require them. During times of transition, there is a lot of focus on what will be different and the changes that will be happening. However, focusing also on all the things that will be staying the same (e.g. the school, where they have assembly, which toilet they use, their friends, where they eat dinner etc.) can support children's anxiety and support them to see that there are many *more* things that will stay the same than those that will change.

It can also be useful for children who require transition booklets, to include the whole-class transition social story so it can be read at home with families over the summer holidays.

Robust and detailed transition meetings: It is vital that during these meetings, all strategies, provision and supporting documents are shared with the new class teacher, including documents such as One Page Profiles. It can include strategies that have been used with success during the year for individuals or groups of children, for example giving responsibilities, morning routine, morning meet and greets, use of visuals/task plans/now and next sheets in lessons, workstations/areas in class, use of adults to best support them in class etc.

Transition day: Before transition day in the summer term, it can support a positive day if any bespoke provision is in place for individuals/groups. For example, do they usually have a workstation in class? Do they usually have a meet and greet? Do they work best when they have a task plan for the morning routine? Do they need an adult to go through the task individually once the class has started their independent task, and so on?

September training day: As adults working in schools, we all know that anxious feeling of coming back to school after the long summer holidays and despite all the above provision being put in place for individuals in the summer term to support a positive transition to their new class, six weeks is still a long time for children to be at home. Most schools have a training day first day back in the autumn term which can be a great time to give individuals a phone call to ask briefly about their holidays, to let them know that you are looking forward to seeing them and to remind them what they will be doing when they come in. They may also have thought of more questions over the summer, so this also gives them an opportunity to get answers to these questions.

Primary to secondary school: The move from a primary setting to a secondary one can be significant for children. Running a transition group for year 6 children who may find the move a challenge can be helpful. This intervention can include discussions around what they are looking forward to about secondary school, what worries they have and any questions they have (which, where possible/appropriate, could be sent to the secondary schools to answer).

As discussed in previous chapters, children with DLD can unintentionally come across in class like they have not listened or are being disrespectful in their responses. Although this is usually not the case, in secondary schools where they have several different teachers each day, they can find themselves in trouble and/or being given consequences for this behaviour. To support them with this, this intervention time could also be used to develop and record talk stems that they can take with them to help them to ask for help if they need it, including alternative phrases that can be used to avoid getting into trouble.

For example:

> Instead of: *'What did you say we have to do?'*
> Say: *'Could you please repeat the instruction?'*
>
> Instead of: *'I don't get it!'*
> Say; *'I understand the bit about ... but can you please remind me what to do after that?'*

Sharing documents: Ensuring that all documents are sent to the child's new school is essential. All schools pass on levels and academic documents, but it is also important to share documents such as the One Page Profiles, so the new members of staff know all about the child, including what they like, what helps them to learn but also what doesn't help and any triggers for them if appropriate.

Parents, Carers and Families

Families of children with DLD can also feel anxiety around times of transition. If their child has additional needs and has historically found transitions a challenge and a highly anxious time, it is likely that families will also be feeling worried and it is reasonable (and expected) that they will want to speak to the new teacher. Families will want to ensure that their new teacher has all the information and to be reassured that they know their child and what provisions to put in place for them to best support the transition.

Therefore, it can be beneficial to provide families with all the information around transition so they can feel reassured themselves. This also means that they will be able to support their child over the summer holidays, allowing their child to be fully prepared and excited to begin their new school year.

This support for families may include:

- **Transition booklet and social story:** Include information about how to support their child using these documents with the transition booklet. For example, the purpose of these documents and how often to look at the booklet and read the social story together.
- **Meet the teacher sheet:** Including this in the documents sent home can support parental anxiety as well as enable the adult to look through this with their child if wanted at various points throughout the summer holidays. Again, information sent home about this document can support families. For example, what the purpose is, how they can use it and any activities they can do linked to it, for example make their own 'Meet the Student' sheet for their teacher.
- **Meet the teacher opportunities for families:** Creating as many opportunities as possible to speak to any families of children who have additional needs or who are

showing heightened anxiety during transition periods, can be beneficial for the family, the child and the teacher. This may be done by offering a 'drop-in' session, arranging a meeting or organising a phone call where the family can tell you all about their child, any needs they have and ask any questions they may have. Being fully prepared for this meeting (e.g. knowing their child's needs, what they need in class etc.) can put the families' minds at ease as they can see that you have taken the time to find the information and are prepared to ensure that everything is in place for them in September.

Ensuring that these meetings happen can also mean that the conversations about the new school year and new teacher over the summer are positive and when children ask their families questions about the new year, rather than the response being a negative one which could escalate the anxiety in both the adult and the child, the response is more likely to be a positive one where the adults can answer their child's questions and feel positive about the new teacher, de-escalating any worries.

- **Worry and anxiety resources:** Depending on the child and the family, it may be helpful to send home some strategies to support worry and anxiety over the summer holidays.
- **September training day:** The phone call that takes place for the child on the training day (as described in the targeted/specialist section) is as much for the adult at home as it is for the child. This phone call communicates to the family that you care about their child and that you have taken the time to help them to feel reassured and happy/excited to come to school the following day.

Examples of a transition social story, the 'Meet the Teacher' sheet and talk stems for secondary school can be found on in the resources section at the end of this chapter.

Reflection: Consider the transition process in your school or setting and the support that you give both children and families. Is there anything extra you could do to support this highly anxious time? Could primary and secondary schools work together to create more links to support this process?

Key Takeaways from Chapter 5

- Transition is an anxious time for all, including families and as much **careful planning prior to transition** should take place to prevent anxiety.
- Creating a **safe and secure environment** and building **trusting relationships** to promote a sense of belonging are the two most important aspects when considering transition.
- **Communication is key** as a lot of the anxiety comes from the unknown. Keeping children 'in the loop' and sharing as much information as possible about the transition process will support a smoother and more positive process.
- Positive **links between primary and secondary** schools can be hugely beneficial for all.

References

Gough Kenyon, S.M., Palikara, O. and Lucas, R.M. (2022). Predictors of school concern across the transition to secondary school with developmental language disorder and low language ability: A longitudinal developmental cascade analysis. *International Journal of Language & Communication Disorders*, *57*(6), pp. 1368–1380.

Gray, C. (2015). *The New Social Story Book. Revised & Expanded. 15th Anniversary Edition*. Future Horizons.

Leaver, V. (2023) Developmental Language Disorder in secondary school. The Education Hub. Available at Developmental Language Disorder in secondary school – THE EDUCATION HUB [accessed 31 May 2024].

McKibben, S. (2014) The two-minute relationship builder. Available at The Two-Minute Relationship Builder (ascd.org) [accessed 17 June 2024].

McLeod, S. (2007). Maslow's hierarchy of needs. *Simply Psychology*, *1*(1–18).

Mould, K. (2021) EEF Blog: Supporting pupils through transitions – a trio of challenges. Available at EEF Blog: Supporting pupils through transitions – a trio of ... | EEF (educationendowmentf oundation.org.uk) [accessed 31 May 2024].

White, J. (2020). Supporting Children's Mental Health and Wellbeing at Transition from Primary to Secondary School: Evidence review. Health Scotland.

Chapter 5

Resources Section

Transition Social Story

Moving On

In September, all children will move into a new class with their friends.

It can feel make us feel excited and also a bit nervous.
This is okay.

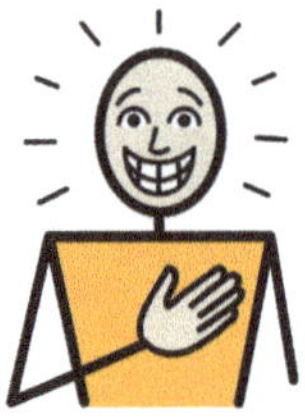

There will be lots of things that stay the same.
There will be some things that change.

My teacher will make sure that we know about the things that will change.

It is okay to ask my teacher any questions that I have.

We will have lots of fun in our new class learning lots of new things.

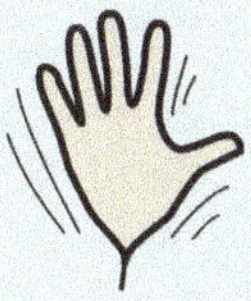

Meet The Teacher!

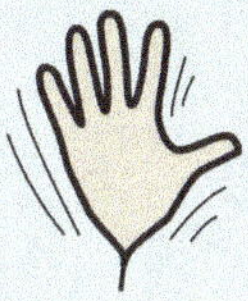

ADD PHOTO

My Name is:

I really enjoy

My favourite animal is

My favourite holiday destination is

In school I love to

I can't wait to meet you and get to know all about you!

Support Sheet for Secondary School

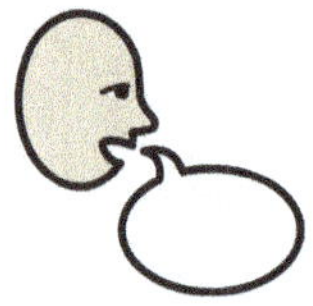

How I Can Ask for Help

Problem	What I can say
Understanding instructions	Can you please repeat the instruction? I understood the first bit but could you please repeat what to do after that?
Not knowing what a word means	Can you please tell me what …… means? Can I please get a dictionary to check the meaning?
Friendships	I am unsure what you mean, can you explain it? Could you help me sort out an argument as I am finding it difficult.
Understanding or remembering questions	Could you please repeat the question? Would you mind writing the question down for me because that helps me? Could I please have a little thinking time?
Answering questions/ speaking to others	Could I please write my ideas down to help me remember them? Could you let me know the question in advance, so I have time to make notes? Could you give me a little extra time to say my sentence?
People understanding	I have DLD so I can find somethings a little more difficult (If have a diagnosis). I can find it difficult to hold information in my head. It can sometimes take me a little time to say a sentence so please be patient with me. Sometimes I don't understand things so am I okay to ask?

Conclusion

Let's start the conversation about DLD and spread the word!

Although, on average, Developmental Language Disorder affects 2–3 children in every mainstream classroom and that the prevalence rate is similar to that of dyslexia (and more prevalent than autism), the majority of pupils in our schools with DLD are currently either undiagnosed or misdiagnosed.

In the current educational climate of increasing challenge in our curriculum, results-driven and fast-paced classrooms, ever-increasing workloads for teachers, a shortage of funding and adults in schools and a gradual increase in need, it is more important than ever to create inclusive classrooms with minimum impact on workload, but which provide the greatest gains for pupils.

By creating a safe and happy classroom environment where relationships are positive and children's behaviours are met with playfulness, acceptance, curiosity and empathy, we are allowing pupils to be themselves, to ask questions without the worry of being reprimanded and ensuring that they are settled and excited to learn.

By considering how language is taught and creating a vocabulary-rich environment which prioritises oral rehearsal, we are ensuring that pupils are developing the tools and the language they need to be successful inside and outside of the classroom.

By ensuring that all pupils have the scaffolds they need to access their lessons (including the use of visuals to support communication, learning and to reduce anxiety) and by considering particularly tricky times for pupils, *all* children can reach their potential.

Taking a holistic approach, including the pupils, all adults they work with daily and their families (particularly as DLD is a genetic condition) is of great benefit. Having a 'team' of trusted adults all working towards the same goal supports the children to feel understood, valued and happy.

The purpose of this book is *not* to recommend a complete change in educational settings and much of the content will not be new to most educators. The purpose of this book is to build on teachers' knowledge and to show how the smallest of *tweaks*

DOI: 10.4324/9781032717869-6

made to the whole-school approach and the learning environment daily can have a significant impact on students.

Because both educators and families are familiar with more well-known conditions such as autism, ADHD or dyslexia, there are certain behaviours observed in pupils that will trigger a conversation about that particular condition. When a child has a persistent difficulty understanding and/or using language, struggles to follow instructions, finds it a challenge to formulate sentences to express themselves, has difficulties with friendships and/or presents with challenging behaviour, let's start the conversation about Developmental Language Disorder.

Consider the examples throughout this book and think about the children that you work with in your setting. Let's not wait for the end of long waiting lists, let's not misdiagnose children who have an unmet speech, language and communication need, but let's start the conversation about DLD and let's develop inclusive classrooms for *all* children so, diagnosis or not, *all* children's needs are catered for, *all* children are able to achieve success and *all* children have great lives.

Index

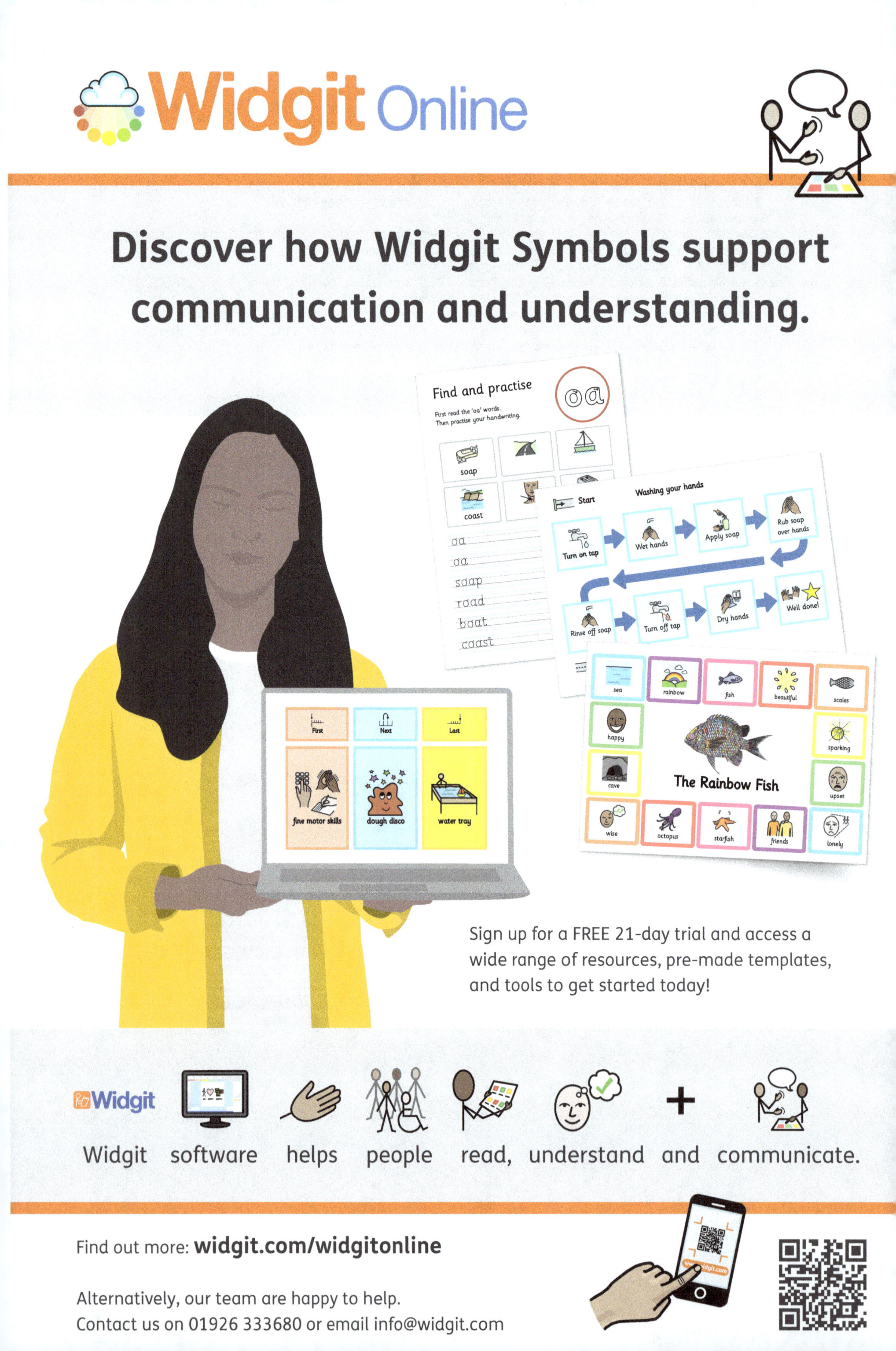
Widgit Online
Discover how Widgit Symbols support communication and understanding.
Sign up for a FREE 21-day trial and access a wide range of resources, pre-made templates, and tools to get started today!
Widgit software helps people read, understand and communicate.
Find out more: widgit.com/widgitonline
Alternatively, our team are happy to help.
Contact us on 01926 333680 or email info@widgit.com

www.ingramcontent.com/pod-product-compliance
Lightning Source LLC
Chambersburg PA
CBHW080909230426
43664CB00017B/2763